studysync®

Reading & Writing Companion

Justice Served

studysync

studysync.com

Send all inquiries to:
BookheadEd Learning, LLC
610 Daniel Young Drive
Sonoma, CA 95476

Cover, ©iStock.com/DNY59, ©iStock.com/Alllex, ©iStock.com/alexey_boldin, ©iStock.com/skegbydave

7 8 9 LWI 21 20 19 18 C

STUDENT GUIDE

GETTING STARTED

Welcome to the StudySync Reading and Writing Companion! In this booklet, you will find a collection of readings based on the theme of the unit you are studying. As you work through the readings, you will be asked to answer questions and perform a variety of tasks designed to help you closely analyze and understand each text selection. Read on for an explanation of

CORE ELA TEXTS

In each Core ELA Unit you will read texts and text excerpts that share a common theme, despite their different genres, time periods, and authors. Each reading encourages a closer look with questions and a short writing assignment.

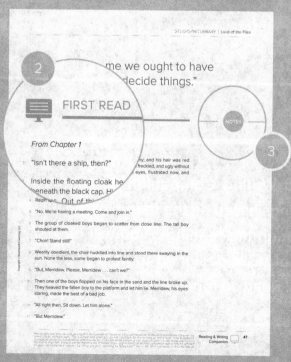

1 INTRODUCTION

An Introduction to each text provides historical context for your reading as well as information about the author. You will also learn about the genre of the excerpt and the year in which it was written.

2 FIRST READ

During your first reading of each excerpt, you should just try to get a general idea of the content and message of the reading. Don't worry if there are parts you don't understand or words that are unfamiliar to you. You'll have an opportunity later to dive deeper into the text.

3 NOTES

Many times, while working through the activities after each text, you will be asked to **annotate** or **make annotations** about what you are reading. This means that you should highlight or underline words in the text and use the "Notes" column to make comments or jot down any questions you may have. You may also want to note any unfamiliar vocabulary words here.

THINK QUESTIONS

These questions will ask you to start thinking critically about the text, asking specific questions about its purpose, and making connections to your prior knowledge and reading experiences. To answer these questions, you should go back to the text and draw upon specific evidence that you find there to support your responses. You will also begin to explore some of the more challenging vocabulary words used in the excerpt.

CLOSE READ & FOCUS QUESTIONS

After you have completed the First Read, you will then be asked to go back and read the excerpt more closely and critically. Before you begin your Close Read, you should read through the Focus Questions to get an idea of the concepts you will want to focus on during your second reading. You should work through the Focus Questions by making annotations, highlighting important concepts, and writing notes or questions in the "Notes" column. Depending on instructions from your teacher, you may need to respond online or use a separate piece of paper to start expanding on your thoughts and ideas.

WRITING PROMPT

Your study of each excerpt or selection will end with a writing assignment. To complete this assignment, you should use your notes, annotations, and answers to both the Think and Focus Questions. Be sure to read the prompt carefully and address each part of it in your writing assignment.

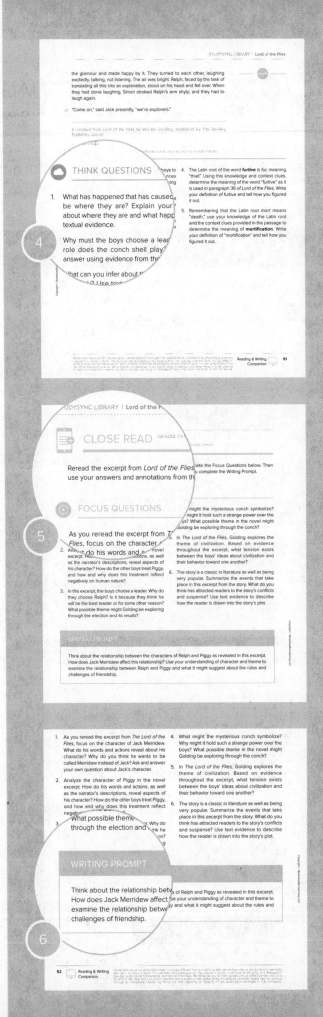

ENGLISH LANGUAGE DEVELOPMENT TEXTS

The English Language Development texts and activities take a closer look at the language choices that authors make to communicate their ideas. Individual and group activities will help develop your understanding of each text.

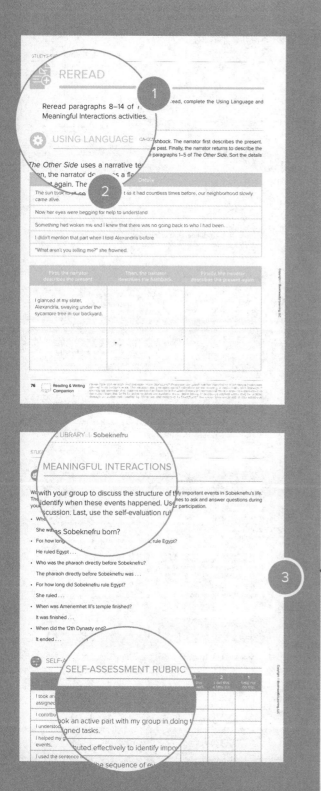

 1 **REREAD**

After you have completed the First Read, you will have two additional opportunities to revisit portions of the excerpt more closely. The directions for each reread will specify which paragraphs or sections you should focus on.

 2 **USING LANGUAGE**

These questions will ask you to analyze the author's use of language and conventions in the text. You may be asked to write in sentence frames, fill in a chart, or you may simply choose between multiple-choice options. To answer these questions, you should read the exercise carefully and go back in the text as necessary to accurately complete the activity.

 3 **MEANINGFUL INTERACTIONS & SELF-ASSESSMENT RUBRIC**

After each reading, you will participate in a group activity or discussion with your peers. You may be provided speaking frames to guide your discussions or writing frames to support your group work. To complete these activities, you should revisit the excerpt for textual evidence and support. When you finish, use the Self-Assessment Rubric to evaluate how well you participated and collaborated.

Copyright © 2016 BookheadEd Learning, LLC

EXTENDED WRITING PROJECT

The Extended Writing Project is your opportunity to explore the theme of each unit in a longer written work. You will draw information from your readings, research, and own life experiences to complete the assignment.

1 WRITING PROJECT

After you have read all of the unit text selections, you will move on to a writing project. Each project will guide you through the process of writing an argumentative, narrative, informative, or literary analysis essay. Student models and graphic organizers will provide guidance and help you organize your thoughts as you plan and write your essay. Throughout the project, you will also study and work on specific writing skills to help you develop different portions of your writing.

2 WRITING PROCESS STEPS

There are five steps in the writing process: **Prewrite**, **Plan**, **Draft**, **Revise**, and **Edit, Proofread, and Publish**. During each step, you will form and shape your writing project so that you can effectively express your ideas. Lessons focus on one step at a time, and you will have the chance to receive feedback from your peers and teacher.

3 WRITING SKILLS

Each Writing Skill lesson focuses on a specific strategy or technique that you will use during your writing project. The lessons begin by analyzing a student model or mentor text, and give you a chance to learn and practice the skill on its own. Then, you will have the opportunity to apply each new skill to improve the writing in your own project.

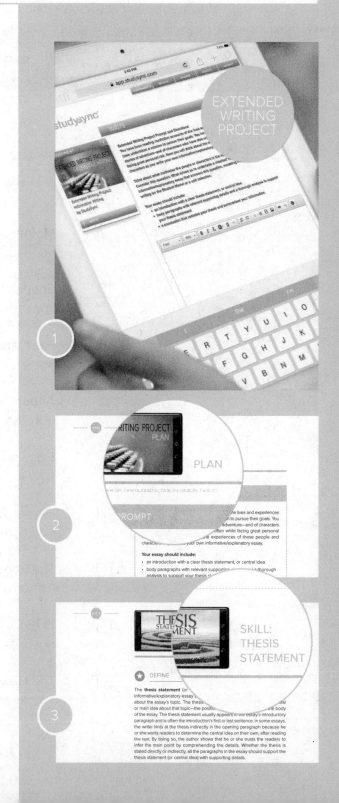

UNIT 3   Why is it essential to defend human rights?

Justice Served

TEXTS

ENGLISH LANGUAGE DEVELOPMENT TEXTS

EXTENDED WRITING PROJECT

127

Text Fulfillment
through
StudySync

MOTHER JONES:

FIERCE FIGHTER FOR WORKERS' RIGHTS

NON-FICTION
Judith Pinkerton Josephson
1996

INTRODUCTION

Born in 1837, Mary Harris Jones, known as Mother Jones, was an American schoolteacher and dressmaker who went on to become a prominent workers' rights activist and community organizer. This excerpt from author Judith Pinkerton Josephson's biography of the fearless crusader describes her groundbreaking demonstrations against unfair child labor practices and her historic 1903 march from Philadelphia to Sagamore Hill, New York, to protest the poor conditions endured by young workers.

"About a sixth of the strikers were children under sixteen."

FIRST READ

From Chapter Nine: The March of the Mill Children

1   "I love children," Mother Jones once told a reporter.

2   In countless shacks and shanties across the country, she had tied the shoes of children, wiped their noses, hugged them while they cried, scrambled to find food for them, fought for their rights. By the turn of the century, almost two million children under the age of sixteen worked in mills, factories, and mines. Images of the child workers Mother Jones had seen stayed with her—the torn, bleeding fingers of the breaker boys, the mill children living on coffee and stale bread.

3   In June 1903, Mother Jones went to Philadelphia, Pennsylvania—the heart of a vast textile industry. About one hundred thousand workers from six hundred different mills were on strike there. The strikers wanted their workweek cut from sixty to fifty-five hours, even if it meant lower wages. About a sixth of the strikers were children under sixteen.

4   Nationwide, eighty thousand children worked in the textile industry. In the South, Mother Jones had seen how dangerous their jobs were. Barefooted little girls and boys reached their tiny hands into the **treacherous** machinery to repair snapped threads or crawled underneath the machinery to oil it. At textile union headquarters, Mother Jones met more of these mill children. Their bodies were bone-thin, with hollow chests. Their shoulders were rounded from long hours spent hunched over the workbenches. Even worse, she saw "some with their hands off, some with the thumb missing, some with their fingers off at the knuckles"—victims of mill accidents.

5   Pennsylvania, like many other states, had laws that said children under thirteen could not work. But parents often lied about a child's age. Poor

Please note that excerpts and passages in the StudySync® library and this workbook are intended as touchstones to generate interest in an author's work. The excerpts and passages do not substitute for the reading of entire texts, and StudySync® strongly recommends that students seek out and purchase the whole literary or informational work in order to experience it as the author intended. Links to online resellers are available in our digital library. In addition, complete works may be ordered through an authorized reseller by filling out and returning to StudySync® the order form enclosed in this workbook.

Reading & Writing Companion

5

families either put their children to work in the mills or starved. Mill owners looked the other way, because child labor was cheap.

6   Mother Jones asked various newspaper publishers why they didn't write about child labor in Pennsylvania. The publishers told her they couldn't, since owners of the mills also owned stock in their newspapers. "Well, I've got stock in these little children," she said, "and I'll arrange a little **publicity.**"

7   Mother Jones, now seventy-three, gathered a large group of mill children and their parents. She led them on a one-mile march from Philadelphia's Independence Square to its courthouse lawn. Mother Jones and a few children climbed up on a platform in front of a huge crowd. She held one boy's arm up high so the crowd could see his **mutilated** hand. "Philadelphia's mansions were built on the broken bones, the quivering hearts, and drooping heads of these children," she said. She lifted another child in her arms so the crowd could see how thin he was.

8   Mother Jones looked directly at the city officials standing at the open windows across the street. "Some day the workers will take possession of your city hall, and when we do, no child will be sacrificed on the altar of profit." Unmoved, the officials quickly closed their windows.

9   Local newspapers and some New York newspapers covered the event. How, Mother Jones wondered, could she draw national attention to the evils of child labor? Philadelphia's famous Liberty Bell, currently on a national tour and drawing huge crowds, gave her an idea. She and the textile union leaders would stage their own tour. They would march the mill children all the way to the president of the United States—Theodore Roosevelt. Mother Jones wanted the president to get Congress to pass a law that would take children out of the mills, mines, and factories, and put them in school.

10 When Mother Jones asked parents for permission to take their children with her, many hesitated. The march from Philadelphia to Sagamore Hill—the president's seaside mansion on Long Island near New York City—would cover 125 miles. It would be a difficult journey. But finally, the parents agreed. Many decided to come along on the march. Other striking men and women offered their help, too.

11 On July 7, 1903, nearly three hundred men, women, and children—followed by four wagons with supplies—began the long march. Newspapers carried daily reports of the march, calling the group "Mother Jones's Industrial Army," or "Mother Jones's Crusaders." The army was led by a fife-and-drum corps of three children dressed in Revolutionary War uniforms. Mother Jones wore her familiar, lace-fringed black dress. The marchers sang and carried flags, banners, and placards that read "We Want to Go to School!" "We Want Time

to Play." **"Prosperity** Is Here, Where is Ours?" "55 Hours or Nothing." "We Only Ask for Justice." "More Schools, Less Hospitals."

12   The temperature rose into the nineties. The roads were dusty, the children's shoes full of holes. Many of the young girls returned home. Some of the marchers walked only as far as the outskirts of Philadelphia. For the hundred or so marchers who remained, this trip was an adventure in spite of the heat. They bathed and swam in brooks and rivers. Each of them carried a knapsack with a knife, fork, tin cup, and plate inside. Mother Jones took a huge pot for cooking meals on the way. Mother Jones also took along costumes, makeup, and jewelry so the children could stop in towns along the route and put on plays about the struggle of textile workers. The fife-and-drum corps gave concerts and passed the hat. People listened and donated money. Farmers met the marchers with wagonloads of fruit, vegetables, and clothes. Railroad engineers stopped their trains and gave them free rides. Hotel owners served free meals.

13   On July 10th, marchers camped across the Delaware river from Trenton, New Jersey. They had traveled about forty miles in three days. At first, police told the group they couldn't enter the city. Trenton mill owners didn't want any trouble. But Mother Jones invited the police to stay for lunch. The children gathered around the cooking pot with their tin plates and cups. The policemen smiled, talked kindly to them, and then allowed them to cross the bridge into Trenton. There Mother Jones spoke to a crowd of five thousand people. That night, the policemen's wives took the children into their homes, fed them, and packed them lunches for the next day's march.

14   By now, many of the children were growing weak. More returned home. Some adults on the march grumbled that Mother Jones just wanted people to notice *her*. They complained to reporters that Mother Jones often stayed in hotels while the marchers camped in hot, soggy tents filled with whining mosquitoes. Sometimes Mother Jones did stay in hotels, because she went ahead of the marchers to arrange for lodging and food in upcoming towns and to get publicity for the march.

15   As the remaining marchers pushed on to Princeton, New Jersey, a thunderstorm struck. Mother Jones and her army camped on the grounds of former President Grover Cleveland's estate. The Clevelands were away, and the caretaker let Mother Jones use the big, cool barn for a **dormitory.**

16   Mother Jones got permission from the mayor of Princeton to speak opposite the campus of Princeton University. Her topic: higher education. She spoke to a large crowd of professors, students, and residents. Pointing to one ten-year-old boy, James Ashworth, she said, "Here's a textbook on economics." The boy's body was stooped from carrying seventy-five-pound bundles of

yarn. "He gets three dollars a week and his sister, who is fourteen, gets six dollars. They work in a carpet factory ten hours a day while the children of the rich are getting their higher education." Her piercing glance swept over the students in the crowd.

17 Mother Jones talked about children who could not read or write because they spent ten hours a day in Pennsylvania's silk mills. Those who hired these child workers used "the hands and feet of little children so they might buy automobiles for their wives and police dogs for their daughters to talk French to." She accused the mill owners of taking "babies almost from the cradle."

18 The next night, the marchers slept on the banks of the Delaware River. In every town, Mother Jones drew on what she did best—speaking—to gather support for her cause. One reporter wrote, "Mother Jones makes other speakers sound like tin cans."

19 Battling heat, rain, and swarms of mosquitoes at night, the marchers arrived in Elizabeth. Socialist party members helped house and feed the weary adults and children. The next morning, two businessmen gave Mother Jones her first car ride. She was delighted with this new "contraption."

20 On July 15, Mother Jones wrote a letter to President Roosevelt. She told him how these poor mill children lived, appealed to him as a father, and asked him to meet with her and the children. President Roosevelt did not answer Mother Jones's letter. Instead, he assigned secret service officers to watch her. They thought she might be a threat to the president. That made her furious.

21 On July 24, after more than two weeks on the road, the marchers reached New York City. By now, just twenty marchers remained. One of them was Eddie Dunphy, a child whose job was to sit on a high stool eleven hours a day handing thread to another worker. For this he was paid three dollars a week. Mother Jones talked about Eddie and about Gussie Rangnew, a child who packed stockings in a factory. She too worked eleven hours a day for pennies.

22 At one meeting, a crowd of thirty thousand gathered. "We are quietly marching toward the president's home," she told the people. "I believe he can do something for these children, although the press declares he cannot."

23 One man wanted the children to have some fun while they were in New York City. Frank Bostick owned the wild animal show at Coney Island, an amusement park and resort. He invited the mill children to spend a day at the park. The children swam in the ocean and played along the beach.

24 When Frank Bostick's wild animal show ended that night, he let Mother Jones speak to the crowd that had attended. To add drama, she had some of the children crawl inside the empty cages. The smells of sawdust and animals

hung in the air. But instead of lions and tigers, the cages held children. The children gripped the iron bars and solemnly stared out at the crowd while Mother Jones spoke.

25 "We want President Roosevelt to hear the wail of the children who never have a chance to go to school, but work eleven and twelve hours a day in the textile mills of Pennsylvania," she said, "who weave the carpets that he and you walk upon; and the lace curtains in your windows, and the clothes of the people."

26 She continued, "In Georgia where children work day and night in the cotton mills they have just passed a bill to protect songbirds. What about the little children from whom all song is gone?" After Mother Jones finished speaking, the crowd sat in stunned silence. In the distance, a lone lion roared.

27 The grueling walk had taken almost three weeks. Mother Jones had written the president twice with no answer. On July 29, she took three young boys to Sagamore Hill, where the president was staying. But the secret service stopped them at the mansion's gates. The president would not see them.

28 The group returned to New York City. Discouraged, Mother Jones reported her failure to the newspapers. Most of the marchers decided to return home. She stayed on briefly with the three children. Once more, she wrote President Roosevelt: "The child of today is the man or woman of tomorrow....I have with me three children who have walked one hundred miles.... If you decide to see these children, I will bring them before you at any time you may set."

29 The president's secretary replied that the president felt that child labor was a problem for individual states to solve. "He is a brave guy when he wants to take a gun out and fight other grown people," said Mother Jones in disgust, "but when those children went to him, he could not see them."

30 In early August, Mother Jones finally took the last three children home. Soon after, the textile workers gave up and ended their strike. Adults and children went back to work, their working conditions unchanged.

31 Though she had not met with the president, Mother Jones had drawn the attention of the nation to the problem of child labor. She became even more of a national figure. Within a few years, Pennsylvania, New York, New Jersey, and other states did pass tougher child labor laws. The federal government finally passed a child labor law (part of the Fair Labor Standards Act) in 1938—thirty-five years after the march of the mill children.

NOTES

THINK QUESTIONS CA-CCSS: CA.RI.7.1, CA.L.7.4a, CA.L.7.4b, CA.L.7.4d

1. Refer to several details in paragraphs 2-4 to support your understanding of why Mother Jones was concerned for the safety of children working in the textile industry.

2. Use details to write two or three sentences describing how Mother Jones got the idea for the march of the mill children and what her goal was. Cite evidence from paragraph 9.

3. What happened when Mother Jones tried to meet with President Roosevelt at Sagamore Hill? Support your answer with evidence from the text.

4. By remembering that the Latin suffix *-ity* means "the state of," use context to determine the meaning of the word **publicity** as it is used in paragraph 6 of *Mother Jones: Fierce Fighter For Workers' Rights*. Write your definition of "publicity" and tell how you determined the meaning of the word.

5. Use context to determine the meaning of the word **mutilated** as it is used in paragraph 7 of *Mother Jones: Fierce Fighter For Workers' Rights*. Write your definition of "mutilated" and explain the context clues you used to figure out its meaning. Then confirm your definition in a print or digital dictionary.

CLOSE READ

CA-CCSS: CA.RI.7.1, CA.RI.7.3, CA.RI.7.4, CA.L.7.4c, CA.L.7.5a, CA.L.7.6, CA.W.7.2a, CA.W.7.2b, CA.W.7.2c, CA.W.7.2d, CA.W.7.2f, CA.W.7.4, CA.W.7.5, CA.W.7.6, CA.W.7.10

Reread the excerpt from *Mother Jones: Fierce Fighter For Workers' Rights.* As you reread, complete the Focus Questions below. Then use your answers and annotations from the questions to help you complete the Writing Prompt.

FOCUS QUESTIONS

1. In an attempt to influence city officials, Mother Jones uses figurative language and negative connotations to imply that children are being abused so that mill owners can make money. Identify the figurative phrase in paragraph 8 and two words that convey a negative connotation. Then analyze how this phrase affects the meaning of the economic term "profit." Use context or a dictionary to help you analyze the words. Highlight evidence in the text and make annotations to explain your choices.

2. In paragraph 10, how did Mother Jones use her ideas to influence the actions and ideas of some of the mill children's parents? Highlight evidence in the text and make annotations to support your response.

3. In paragraph 12, how did Mother Jones use the children, as well as the events illustrating the children's plight, to influence the opinions and ideas of others? Highlight evidence in the text and annotate your reasoning.

4. What action at the wild animal show, described in paragraphs 23-26, did Mother Jones take to make the plight of the children more dramatic? Highlight textual evidence and make annotations to support your explanation.

5. What evidence in the last paragraph suggests that Mother Jones was successful in defending human rights, particularly the rights of child workers? Highlight evidence in the text and make annotations to support your answer.

WRITING PROMPT

How is Mother Jones like other individuals you have heard of who have worked hard to defend human rights? Begin with a clear thesis statement to introduce this topic. Think about the ways in which Mother Jones attempted to influence individuals, ideas, and events, especially the ideas of government officials. Organize and cite specific evidence from the text to support your response. Use transitions within your body paragraphs to show the relationships among your ideas. Choose specific vocabulary from the text and use precise language to deliver your ideas. Then, summarize these ideas in a concluding statement that leads logically from the information you have presented.

Please note that excerpts and passages in the StudySync® library and this workbook are intended as touchstones to generate interest in an author's work. The excerpts and passages do not substitute for the reading of entire texts, and StudySync® strongly recommends that students seek out and purchase the whole literary or informational work in order to experience it as the author intended. Links to online resellers are available in our digital library. In addition, complete works may be ordered through an authorized reseller by filling out and returning to StudySync® the order form enclosed in this workbook.

Reading & Writing Companion   11

SPEECH TO THE YOUNG:
SPEECH TO THE PROGRESS-TOWARD

POETRY
Gwendolyn Brooks
1932

INTRODUCTION

A highly regarded and widely admired poet, Gwendolyn Brooks was the poet laureate of Illinois and the first African American to win the Pulitzer Prize. In her poem "Speech to the Young: Speech to the Progress-Toward," the speaker gives wise advice to young people about how to live life.

"Live not for the-end-of-the-song."

 FIRST READ

1 Say to them,
2 say to the down-**keepers,**
3 the sun-**slappers,**
4 the self-**soilers,**
5 the **harmony-hushers,**
6 "even if you are not ready for day
7 it cannot always be night."
8 You will be right.
9 For that is the hard home-run.

10 Live not for battles won.
11 Live not for the-end-of-the-song.
12 Live in the along.

"Speech to the Young: Speech to the Progress Forward" by Gwendolyn Brooks.
Reprinted by Consent of Brooks Permissions.

Please note that excerpts and passages in the StudySync® library and this workbook are intended as touchstones to generate interest in an author's work. The excerpts and passages do not substitute for the reading of entire texts, and StudySync® strongly recommends that students seek out and purchase the whole literary or informational work in order to experience it as the author intended. Links to online resellers are available in our digital library. In addition, complete works may be ordered through an authorized reseller by filling out and returning to StudySync® the order form enclosed in this workbook.

Reading & Writing
Companion

13

THINK QUESTIONS
CA-CCSS: CA.RL.7.1, CA.L.7.4a, CA.L.7.4b, CA.L.7.4d, CA.L.7.5a

1. What evidence is there in the first stanza of the poem that the speaker is giving advice? To whom is the speaker giving advice? Cite textual evidence to support your answer.

2. Who are the young supposed to address? What are they supposed to say? Cite textual evidence to support your answer.

3. How does the speaker want young people to live? Cite textual evidence to support your response.

4. Use context to determine the meaning of **slappers** as it is used in line 3. Write down the meaning. What do you think the connotation of "sun-slappers" is? Cite clues to demonstrate how you determined the meaning of the word.

5. The word **harmony** in line 5 comes from the Greek word *harmos*, which means "a fitting" or "a combining of parts into a whole." Based on the Greek root of the word, what do you think "harmony" means in the context of the poem? What do the "harmony-hushers" want to do? Cite clues to show how you figured out the meaning of the word. Then confirm your meaning of "harmony" in a print or digital dictionary.

CLOSE READ CA-CCSS: CA.RL.7.1, CA.RL.7.2, CA.RL.7.4, CA.L.7.5a, CA.W.7.1

Reread the poem "Speech to the Young: Speech to the Progress-Toward." As you reread, complete the Focus Questions below. Then use your answers and annotations from the questions to help you complete the Writing Prompt.

FOCUS QUESTIONS

1. Brooks uses the repetition of words in the first two lines of the poem to make clear that she is lumping together the people mentioned in lines 2-5. Highlight the repetition in lines 1 and 2, and make annotations explaining how this repetition unites the people.

2. Highlight the use of figurative language in lines 6-7. What do these metaphors mean? How do they support one of the themes of the poem? Make annotations explaining your response.

3. Brooks uses alliteration and figurative language in line 9. Highlight the examples of alliteration and figurative language. What is Brooks trying to say through these poetic elements? Make annotations explaining Brooks's message, or theme.

4. In the last stanza, what metaphor does Brooks use to represent the past? What metaphor does she use to represent the future? Highlight the words, and make annotations explaining how the metaphors might relate to the theme of progress toward racial equality and social justice.

5. Highlight the metaphor that Brooks uses in line 12. Make annotations explaining its meaning. How might this metaphor relate to a theme of progress in social justice?

WRITING PROMPT

How does the use of alliteration and other forms of repetition help Gwendolyn Brooks develop her themes in "Speech to the Young: Speech to the Progress-Toward"? How does the use of figurative language, such as metaphors, contribute to the development of the themes? Use your understanding of poetic elements to determine the themes that emerge in this poem. Support your writing with specific evidence from the text.

Please note that excerpts and passages in the StudySync® library and this workbook are intended as touchstones to generate interest in an author's work. The excerpts and passages do not substitute for the reading of entire texts, and StudySync® strongly recommends that students seek out and purchase the whole literary or informational work in order to experience it as the author intended. Links to online resellers are available in our digital library. In addition, complete works may be ordered through an authorized reseller by filling out and returning to StudySync® the order form enclosed in this workbook.

Reading & Writing Companion   **15**

FLESH AND BLOOD SO CHEAP:
THE TRIANGLE FIRE AND ITS LEGACY

NON-FICTION
Albert Marrin
2011

INTRODUCTION

The Triangle Shirtwaist Factory fire in 1911 was the most lethal workplace tragedy in American history until the attack on the World Trade Center on September 11, 2001. The lower Manhattan blaze killed 146 workers, most of them young, female immigrants of Jewish and Italian descent. Author Albert Marrin traces the history of the garment industry, exploring the immigrant experience of the early 1900s, including the sweatshop conditions many new arrivals to America were forced to endure. The Triangle fire prompted activists to lobby for reforms, resulting in improved safety standards and working conditions that we now take for granted.

"Seconds later, the fire leaped out of control."

FIRST READ

Excerpt from Chapter V

Holocaust

1   We will never know for sure what started the Triangle Fire. Most likely, a cutter flicked a hot ash or tossed a live cigarette butt into a scrap bin. Whatever the cause, survivors said the first sign of trouble was smoke pouring from beneath a cutting table.

2   Cutters flung buckets of water at the smoking spot, without effect. Flames shot up, **igniting** the line of hanging paper patterns. "They began to fall on the layers of thin goods underneath them," recalled cutter Max Rothen. "Every time another piece dropped, light scraps of burning fabric began to fly around the room. They came down on the other tables and they fell on the machines. Then the line broke and the whole string of burning patterns fell down." A foreman ran for the hose on the stairway wall. Nothing! No water came. The hose had not been connected to the **standpipe.** Seconds later, the fire leaped out of control.

3   Yet help was already on the way. At exactly 4:45 p.m., someone pulled the eighth-floor fire alarm. In less than two minutes, the horse-drawn vehicles of Engine Company 72 arrived from a firehouse six blocks away. The moment they arrived, the firefighters unloaded their equipment and prepared to swing into action. As they did, the area pumping station raised water pressure in the hydrants near the Asch Building. Other units soon arrived from across the Lower East Side with more equipment.

4   Meanwhile, workers on the eighth-floor rang furiously for the two passenger elevators. Safety experts have always advised against using elevators in a fire. Heat can easily damage their machinery, leaving trapped passengers dangling in space, to burn or **suffocate.** Despite the danger, the operators

Please note that excerpts and passages in the StudySync® library and this workbook are intended as touchstones to generate interest in an author's work. The excerpts and passages do not substitute for the reading of entire texts, and StudySync® strongly recommends that students seek out and purchase the whole literary or informational work in order to experience it as the author intended. Links to online resellers are available in our digital library. In addition, complete works may be ordered through an authorized reseller by filling out and returning to StudySync® the order form enclosed in this workbook.

Reading & Writing
Companion

17

made several trips, saving scores of workers before heat bent the elevators' tracks and put them out of action.

5 Those who could not board elevators rushed the stairway door. They caused a pile up so that those in front could not open the door. Whenever someone tried to get it open, the crowd pinned her against it. "All the girls were falling on me and they squeezed me to the door," Ida Willensky recalled. "Three times I said to the girls, 'Please, girls, let me open the door. Please!' But they would not listen to me." Finally, cutter Louis Brown barged through the crowd and forced the door open.

6 Workers, shouting, crying, and gasping for air, slowly made their way downstairs. There were no lights in the stairway, so they had to grope their way in darkness. A girl fell; others fell on top of her, blocking the stairs until firefighters arrived moments later. Yet everyone who took the stairway from the eighth floor got out alive, exiting through the Washington Place doors. Those on the ninth floor were not so lucky.

. . .

7 Those who reached the ninth-floor stairway door found it locked. This was not unusual, as employers often locked doors to discourage latecomers and keep out union organizers. "My God, I am lost!" cried Margaret Schwartz as her hair caught fire. Nobody who went to that door survived, nor any who reached the windows.

8 With a wave of fire rolling across the room, workers rushed to the windows, only to meet more fire. Hot air expands. Unless it escapes, pressure will keep building, eventually blowing a hole even in a heavy iron container like a boiler. Heat and pressure blew out the eight-floor windows. Firefighters call the result "lapping in" —that is sucking flames into open windows above. That is why you see black scorch marks on the wall above the window of a burnt out room.

9 With fire advancing from behind and flames rising before them, people knew they were doomed. Whatever they did meant certain death. By remaining in the room, they chose death by fire or suffocation. Jumping ninety-five feet to the ground meant death on the sidewalk. We cannot know what passed through the minds of those who decided to jump. Yet their thinking, in those last moments of life, may have gone like this: If I jump, my family will have a body to identify and bury, but if I stay in this room, there will be nothing left.

10 A girl clung to a window frame until flames from the eighth floor lapped in, burning her face and setting fire to her hair and clothing. She let go. Just then, Frances Perkins reached the scene from her friend's town house on the north

side of Washington Square. "Here they come," onlookers shouted as Engine Company 72 reined in their horses. "Don't jump; stay there." Seconds later, Hook and Ladder Company 20 arrived.

11 Firefighters charged into the building, stretching a hose up the stairways as they went. At the sixth-floor landing, they connected it to the standpipe. Reaching the eighth floor, they crawled into the **inferno** on their bellies, under the rising smoke, with their hose. Yet nothing they did could save those at the windows. Photos of the portable towers show streams of water playing on the top three floors. (A modern high-pressure pumper can send water as high as one thousand feet.) Plenty of water got through the windows, but not those with people standing in them. A burst of water under high pressure would have hurled them backward, into the flames.

12 Hoping to catch jumpers before they hit the ground, firefighters held up life nets, sturdy ten-foot-square nets made of rope. It was useless. A person falling from the ninth floor struck with a force equal to eleven thousand pounds. Some jumpers bounced off the nets, dying when they hit the ground; others tore the nets, crashing through to the pavement. "The force was so great it took men off their feet," said Captain Howard Ruch of Engine Company 18. "Trying to hold the nets, the men turned somersaults. The men's hands were bleeding, the nets were torn and some caught fire" from burning clothing. Officers, fearing their men would be struck by falling bodies, ordered the nets removed. The **aerial** ladders failed, too, reaching only to the sixth floor. Desperate jumpers tried to grab hold of a rung on the way down, missed, and landed on the sidewalk.

. . .

13 Onlookers saw many dreadful sights, none more so than the end of a love affair. A young man appeared at a window. Gently, he helped a young woman step onto the windowsill, held her away from the building—and let go. He helped another young woman onto the windowsill. "Those of us who were looking saw her put her arms around him and kiss him," Shepherd wrote. "Then he held her out into space and dropped her. But quick as a flash he was on the windowsill himself.... He was brave enough to help the girl he loved to a quicker death, after she had given him a goodbye kiss."

. . .

14 By 5:15 p.m., exactly thirty-five minutes after flames burst from beneath a cutting table, firefighters had brought the blaze under control. An hour later, Chief Croker made his inspection. He found that the Asch Building had no damage to its structure. Its walls were in good shape; so were the floors. It had passed the test. It was fireproof.

NOTES

15   The woodwork, furniture, cotton goods, and people who worked in it were not. Of the 500 Triangle employees who reported for work that day, 146 died. Of these, sixteen men were identified. The rest were women or bodies and body parts listed as "unidentified." The Triangle Fire was New York's worst workplace disaster up to that time. Only the September 11, 2001, terrorist attacks on the twin towers of the World Trade Center took more (about 2,500) lives.

Excerpted from *Flesh and Blood So Cheap: The Triangle Fire and Its Legacy* by Albert Marrin, published by Alfred A. Knopf.

THINK QUESTIONS   CA-CCSS: CA.RI.7.1, CA.L.7.4a, CA.L.7.4b, CA.SL.7.1a, CA.SL.7.1d, CA.SL.7.1c, CA.SL.7.3, CA.SL.7.5

1. Refer to several details in the first two paragraphs to support your understanding of how the Triangle Fire likely started and how the fire spread on the eighth floor.

2. Write two or three sentences describing what caused the windows to blow out on the eighth floor and how this affected the ninth floor above. Cite specific textual evidence from paragraph 8.

3. What did firefighters attempt to do to help those who jumped from the ninth floor? Why were these efforts not successful? Support your answer with evidence from paragraph 12 of the text.

4. Use context to determine the meaning of the word **standpipe** as it is used in paragraphs 2 and 11 of *Flesh and Blood So Cheap*. Write your definition of "standpipe" and tell how you determined the meaning of the word.

5. By keeping in mind that the Greek root *aer* means "air" and the Latin suffix *-ial* means "having the characteristics of," use the context clues provided in paragraph 12 to determine the meaning of **aerial** ladders. Write your definition of "aerial" and tell how you got it. Then describe what an aerial ladder would be.

CLOSE READ
CA-CCSS: CA.RI.7.1, CA.RI.7.5, CA.W.7.2.a, CA.W.7.2.b, CA.W.7.4, CA.W.7.5, CA.W.7.6, CA.W.7.10

Reread the excerpt from *Flesh and Blood So Cheap*. As you reread, complete the Focus Questions below. Then use your answers and annotations from the questions to help you complete the Writing Prompt.

FOCUS QUESTIONS

1. Explain how the author uses a cause-and-effect text structure in paragraph 4. Highlight evidence from the text and make annotations to explain your reasoning.

2. In paragraphs 6 and 7, Marrin sets up a comparison-contrast between what happened to the workers on the eighth and ninth floors. What other text structure does he use in sentences 2-4 of paragraph 6? Highlight the transition word in sentence 2, and annotate to label the text structure.

3. What text structure does the author use in paragraph 9? How does this organizational structure contribute to the development of ideas? Highlight evidence and make annotations to explain your answer.

4. In the first three sentences of paragraph 11, the author uses a descriptive text structure at the sentence level. What evidence supports this claim? What would you say is the overall text structure of the paragraph? Highlight evidence from the text and make annotations to support your explanations.

5. Use evidence from paragraphs 2, 6, 7, 14, and 15 to support the claim that the owners of the Triangle Shirtwaist Factory did not do enough to protect workers' rights. Highlight evidence from the text and make annotations to support the claim.

WRITING PROMPT

A legacy of the Triangle Fire described in *Flesh and Blood So Cheap* was the call for laws to protect workers' rights. What evidence is there that the health and safety of workers were not adequately protected at the Triangle Shirtwaist Factory? Begin with a clear thesis statement, and use your understanding of informational text structure to write a short essay to answer the question: Why is it necessary for the government to protect the health and safety of workers? Summarize your points with a strong conclusion, and support your writing with evidence and inferences drawn from the text.

Please note that excerpts and passages in the StudySync® library and this workbook are intended as touchstones to generate interest in an author's work. The excerpts and passages do not substitute for the reading of entire texts, and StudySync® strongly recommends that students seek out and purchase the whole literary or informational work in order to experience it as the author intended. Links to online resellers are available in our digital library. In addition, complete works may be ordered through an authorized reseller by filling out and returning to StudySync® the order form enclosed in this workbook.

Reading & Writing Companion   **21**

ABOUT CÉSAR

NON-FICTION
César Chávez Foundation
2012

INTRODUCTION

César Chávez was a Mexican-American activist who dedicated his life to promoting non-violent approaches to labor reform. He drew on his experiences as a migrant worker to found the National Farm Workers Association with fellow activist, Dolores Huerta in 1962. Through boycotts, hunger strikes, and marches, Chávez and his supporters successfully improved the lives of farmers around the country, and his speeches about justice, community, and education still resonate with community activists and politicians today. President Barack Obama adopted Chávez's most famous motto, "Si, se puede," as his 2008 campaign slogan. This excerpt from the César Chávez Foundation describes union

"The significance of César's life transcends any one cause or struggle."

FIRST READ

Senator Robert F. Kennedy described Cesar Chavez as "one of the heroic figures of our time."

1   A true American hero, Cesar was a civil rights, Latino and farm labor leader; a genuinely religious and spiritual figure; a community organizer and social entrepreneur; a champion of militant nonviolent social change; and a crusader for the environment and consumer rights.

2   A first-generation American, he was born on March 31, 1927, near his family's small homestead in the North Gila River Valley outside Yuma, Arizona. At age 11, his family lost their farm during the Great Depression and became migrant farm workers. Throughout his youth and into adulthood, Cesar traveled the migrant streams throughout California laboring in the fields, orchards and vineyards, where he was exposed to the hardships and injustices of farm worker life.

3   After attending numerous schools as the family migrated, Cesar finished his formal education after the eighth grade and worked the fields full-time to help support his family. Although his formal education ended then, he later satisfied an insatiable intellectual curiosity and was self-taught on an eclectic range of subjects through reading during the rest of his life.

4   Cesar joined the U.S. Navy in 1946, in the aftermath of World War II, and served in the Western Pacific. He returned from the service in 1948 to marry Helen Fabela, whom he met while working in fields and vineyards around Delano. Together they settled in the East San Jose barrio of *Sal Si Puedes* (Get Out if You Can), and had eight children, later enjoying 31 grandchildren.

Please note that excerpts and passages in the StudySync® library and this workbook are intended as touchstones to generate interest in an author's work. The excerpts and passages do not substitute for the reading of entire texts, and StudySync® strongly recommends that students seek out and purchase the whole literary or informational work in order to experience it as the author intended. Links to online resellers are available in our digital library. In addition, complete works may be ordered through an authorized reseller by filling out and returning to StudySync® the order form enclosed in this workbook.

Reading & Writing Companion   **23**

Historic Victories for Union

5   The coming years would bring much more **adversity:** Strikes and boycotts, marches and fasts, victories and defeats. But through it all, Cesar learned and taught others how commitment and sacrifice can set you free from the **constraints** imposed by depending entirely on money and material things.

6   Over four decades, Cesar saw his share of defeats, but also historic victories. Under Cesar, the UFW achieved **unprecedented** gains for farm workers, establishing it as the first successful farm workers union in American history. Among them were:

7   The first genuine collective bargaining agreements between farm workers and growers in American history.

8   The first union contracts requiring rest periods, toilets in the fields, clean drinking water, hand washing facilities, banning discrimination in employment and sexual harassment of women workers, requiring protective clothing against pesticide exposure, prohibiting pesticide spraying while workers are in the fields and outlawing DDT and other dangerous pesticides (years before the U.S. Environmental Protection Agency acted).

9   The first comprehensive union medical (and later dental and vision) benefits for farm workers and their families through a joint union-employer health and welfare fund, the Robert F. Kennedy Medical Plan, which has paid out more than $250 million in benefits.

10 The first and only functioning pension plan for retired farm workers, the Juan de la Cruz Pension Plan, with present assets of more than $100 million.

11 The first union contracts providing for profit sharing and parental leave.

12 Abolishment of the infamous short-handled hoe that crippled generations of farm workers.

13 Extending to farm workers state coverage under unemployment insurance, disability and workers' compensation, as well as federal amnesty rights for immigrants.

14 Because of Cesar and millions of Americans who supported farm workers by boycotting grapes and other products, under then-Gov. Jerry Brown California passed the landmark Agricultural Labor Relations Act of 1975, the nation's first, and still the only, law guaranteeing farm workers the right to organize, choose their own union representative and **negotiate** with their employers.

Cesar Chavez's Legacy

15   The significance of Cesar's life **transcends** any one cause or struggle. He was a unique and humble leader, as well as a great humanitarian and communicator who influenced and inspired millions of Americans from all walks of life. Cesar forged a national and extraordinarily diverse **coalition** for farm worker boycotts, which included students, middle class consumers, trade unionists, religious activists and minorities.

16   Cesar passed away peacefully in his sleep on April 23, 1993 in the small farm worker town of San Luis, Arizona, not far from where he was born 66 years earlier on the family homestead. More than 50,000 people attended his funeral services in Delano, the same community in which he had planted the seeds of social justice decades before.

17   Cesar's motto, "Sí, se puede!" ("Yes, it can be done!"), coined during his 1972 fast in Arizona, embodies the uncommon legacy he left for people around the world. Since his death, hundreds of communities across the nation have named schools, parks, streets, libraries, and other public facilities, as well as awards and scholarships in his honor. His birthday, March 31st, is an official holiday in 10 states. In 1994, President Clinton posthumously awarded Cesar the Presidential Medal of Freedom, the nation's highest civilian honor, at the White House.

18   Cesar liked to say that his job as an organizer was helping ordinary people do extraordinary things. Cesar made everyone, especially the farm workers, feel the jobs they were doing in the movement were very important. It did not matter if they were lawyers working in the courtrooms or cooks in the kitchen feeding the people involved in the strike, he showed the farm workers that they could win against great odds. He gave people the faith to believe in themselves, even if they were poor and unable to receive the best education. Cesar succeeded where so many others failed for 100 years to organize farm workers. He was able to do the impossible by challenging and overcoming the power of one of the country's richest industries in California.

19   As a common man with an uncommon vision, Cesar Chavez stood for equality, justice and dignity for all Americans. His universal principles remain as relevant and inspiring today as they were when he first began his movement.

"About Cesar". Used by permission of The Cesar Chavez Foundation, http://www. chavezfoundation.org/

Please note that excerpts and passages in the StudySync® library and this workbook are intended as touchstones to generate interest in an author's work. The excerpts and passages do not substitute for the reading of entire texts, and StudySync® strongly recommends that students seek out and purchase the whole literary or informational work in order to experience it as the author intended. Links to online resellers are available in our digital library. In addition, complete works may be ordered through an authorized reseller by filling out and returning to StudySync® the order form enclosed in this workbook.

Reading & Writing Companion   25

THINK QUESTIONS   CA-CCSS: CA.RI.7.1, CA.L.7.4a, CA.L.7.4b, CA.L.7.4d

1. Use specific details from paragraphs 1-3 to write three or four sentences summarizing Cesar Chavez's early life before joining the U.S. Navy in 1946.

2. Refer to details from paragraph 8 to support your understanding of how the UFW, under Chavez's leadership, used union contracts to make working conditions safer for farm workers. Cite specific evidence from the text.

3. In the next-to-last paragraph, readers are told that Chavez believed "that his job as an organizer was helping ordinary people do extraordinary things." Write two or three sentences exploring how Chavez did this. Support your answer with textual evidence.

4. Use context clues to determine the meaning of the word **adversity** as it is used in paragraph 5 of "About Cesar." Write your definition of "adversity" and tell how you determined its meaning. Then check the meaning you inferred in a print or digital dictionary.

5. By remembering that the Latin prefix *trans-* means "over" or "across" and the Latin root *scandere* means "to climb," use the context clues provided in the passage to determine the meaning of **transcends** as it is used in paragraph 15 of "About Cesar." Write your definition of "transcends" and tell how you figured out its meaning.

CLOSE READ

CA-CCSS: CA.RI.7.1, CA.RI.7.3, CA.W.7.2a, CA.W.7.2b, CA.W.7.2c, CA.W.7.2d, CA.W.7.2f, CA.W.7.4, CA.W.7.5, CA.W.7.6, CA.W.7.10

Reread the essay "About Cesar." As you reread, complete the Focus Questions below. Then use your answers and annotations from the questions to help you complete the Writing Prompt.

FOCUS QUESTIONS

1. What can a reader infer from the details in paragraph 3 about how life as a migrant farm worker affected Chavez's formal education? What steps did Chavez take to satisfy his intellectual curiosity throughout the rest of his life? Highlight textual evidence and make annotations to explain your responses.

2. Which details in paragraphs 6 and 7 indicate that Chavez was able to have a positive influence on the lives of migrant farm workers through his actions and ideas? Highlight textual evidence and make annotations to explain your choices.

3. Which details in paragraph 14 indicate the influence that Chavez had on legislation by leading millions of American supporters of farm workers in boycotts of grapes and other products? Highlight textual evidence and make annotations to explain your choices.

4. What evidence in paragraph 17 shows that Chavez's influence extended far beyond migrant farm workers? Highlight textual evidence and make annotations to support your explanation.

5. According to paragraph 18, why was Chavez able to succeed in organizing farm workers when so many other organizers had failed? Highlight textual evidence and make annotations to explain your answer.

WRITING PROMPT

Why is "Sí, se puede!" ("Yes, it can be done!") a fitting motto for Cesar Chavez's life and for the influence he had on events, ideas, and the people around him? Why do you think Chavez thought it was important to defend human rights? In crafting your response, begin with a clear thesis statement and use your understanding of informational text elements by analyzing the interaction among people, ideas, and events in the selection. Organize and support your writing with textual evidence, and use precise language and vocabulary from the selection. Use transitions to show the relationships among your ideas, and provide a concluding statement that summarizes your key points.

Please note that excerpts and passages in the StudySync® library and this workbook are intended as touchstones to generate interest in an author's work. The excerpts and passages do not substitute for the reading of entire texts, and StudySync® strongly recommends that students seek out and purchase the whole literary or informational work in order to experience it as the author intended. Links to online resellers are available in our digital library. In addition, complete works may be ordered through an authorized reseller by filling out and returning to StudySync® the order form enclosed in this workbook.

Reading & Writing Companion **27**

ELEGY ON THE DEATH OF CÉSAR CHÁVEZ

POETRY
Rudolfo Anaya
2000

INTRODUCTION

In this poem, Rudolfo Anaya eulogizes César Chávez, who fought for the rights of migrant farm workers in America. The poem celebrates Chávez's life and mourns his death, even as his causes survive.

"How can the morning star die?"

FIRST READ

1   César is dead,
2   And we have wept for him until our eyes are dry.
3   Dry as the fields of California that
4   He loved so well and now lie **fallow.**
5   Dry as the orchards of Yakima, where dark buds
6   Hang on trees and do not blossom.
7   Dry as el Valle de Tejas where people cross
8   Their Foreheads and pray for rain.

9   This earth he loved so well is dry and mourning
10 For César has fallen, our morning star has fallen.

11 The messenger came with the sad news of his death—
12 O, kill the messenger and steal back the life
13 Of this man who was a guide across fields of toil.
14 Kill the day and stop all time, stop la muerte
15 Who has robbed us of our morning star, that
16 Luminous light that greeted workers as they
17 Gathered around the dawn campfires
18 Let the morning light of Quetzacótal and Christian saint
19 Shine again. Let the wings of the Holy Ghost unfold
20 And give back the spirit it took from us in sleep.

21 Across the land we heard las campanas doblando:
22 *Ha muerto César, Ha muerto César.*

23 How can the morning star die? We ask. How can

24 This man who moved like the light of justice die?

25 Hijo de la Virgen de Guadalupe, hombre de la gente,
26 You starved your body so we might know your spirit.

27 The days do carry hope, and the days do carry treason.

28 O, fateful day, April 23, 1993, when our morning
29 Star did not rise and we knew that in his sleep
30 César had awakened to a greater dream.

31 And we, left lost on this dark, dry Earth,
32 Cursed the day la muerte came to claim
33 The light within his noble body.

34 He was a wind of change that swept over our land.
35 From the San Joaquin Valley north to Sacramento
36 From northwest Yakima to el Valle de Tejas
37 From el Valle de San Luis to Midwest fields of corn
38 He loved the land, he loved la gente.

39 His name was a soft breeze to cool the campesino's sweat
40 A scourge on the **oppressors** of the poor.

41 Now he lies dead, and storms still rage around us.
42 The dispossessed walk hopeless streets,
43 Campesinos gather by roadside ditches to sleep,
44 Shrouded by pesticides, unsure of tomorrow,
45 Hounded by **propositions** that keep their children
46 Uneducated in a land grown fat with greed.

47 Yes, the **arrogant** hounds of hate
48 Are loose upon this land again, and César
49 Weeps in the embrace of La Virgen de Guadalupe,
50 Still praying for his people.

51 "Rise, mi gente, rise," he prays.

52 His words echo across the land, like the righteous

53 Thunder of summer storms, like the call of a
54 Warrior preparing for the struggle. I hear his
55 Voice in the fields and orchards, in community halls,
56 In schools, churches, campesino homes and
57 Presidential palaces.
58 "Rise, mi gente, rise."
59 That was his common chant. Rise and organize,

60 Build the House of Workers.
61 Build the House of Justice now!

62 Do not despair in violence and abuse.
63 Rise together and build a new society.
64 Build a new democracy, build equality,
65 And build a dream for all to share.

66 His voice stirs me now, and I rise from my grief.
67 I hear the words of the poet cry:
68 "Peace, peace! He is not dead, he doth not sleep—
69 He hath awakened from the dream of life."

70 I hear César calling for us to gather.

71 I hear the call to a new Huelga,
72 I hear the sound of marching feet
73 The guitarra strums of the New Movimiento
74 The old and young, rich and poor, all move
75 To build the House of Justice of César's dream!

76 The trumpet of righteousness calls us to battle!
77 And the future opens itself like the blossom
78 That is his soul, the fruit of his labor.
79 He calls for us to share in the fruit.

80 "He lives, he wakes—'tis Death is dead, not he;
81 Mourn not for Adonais."

82 Do not weep for César, for he is not dead.
83 He lives in the hearts of those who loved him,
84 Worked and marched and ate with him, and those
85 Who believed in him.

86 His disciples know he is not dead.
87 For in the dawn we see the morning star!
88 El lucero de Dios!
89 Light comes to illuminate the struggle,
90 And bless the work yet to be done.

91 Throughout Aztlán we call the young to gather;
92 Rise and put aside violence and temptations.
93 Rise and be swept up by the truth of his deeds,
94 Rise not against each other, but for each other,
95 Rise against the oppressors who take your seat
96 And labor and sell it cheap.

NOTES

97   "Rise, mi gente, rise!"

98   Our César has not died!
99   He is the light of the new day.
100 He is the rain that renews **parched** fields.
101 He is the hope that builds the House of Justice.
102 He is with us! Here! Today!
103 Listen to his voice in the wind.
104 He is the spirit of Hope,
105 A movement building to sweep away oppression!
106 His spirit guides us in the struggle.
107 Let us join his spirit to ours!
108 Sing with me. Sing all over this land!

109 "Rise, mi gente, rise!

110 Rise, mi gente, rise!"

From "Elegy on the Death of Cesar Chavez". Copyright © 2000 by Rudolfo Anaya. Published by Cinco Punto Press. By permission of Susan Bergholz Literary Services, New York, NY and Lamy, NM. All rights reserved.

THINK QUESTIONS   CA-CCSS: CA.RL.7.1, CA.L.7.4a, CA.L.7.4d

1. What language confirms that this is an elegy, a poem about someone who has died? Cite textual evidence to support your answer.

2. What terms of praise does Rudolfo Anaya apply to Chavez in the elegy? Cite evidence from the text to support your answer.

3. What chant does the poet repeat in the poem? Cite evidence to explain why the chant is important to the theme (or message) of the poem.

4. Use context clues to determine the meaning of **fallow** as it is used in line 4 of the first stanza. Write the meaning of the word. Cite clues to demonstrate how you got your answer.

5. Use context clues to determine the meaning of **oppressors** as it is used in lines 40 and 95. Write the meaning of the word. Cite clues from lines 40 and 95 and surrounding lines to indicate how you inferred the meaning of the word. Then use a print or digital dictionary to confirm or revise your definition.

CLOSE READ

CA-CCSS: CA.RL.7.1, CA.RL.7.2, CA.RL.7.4, CA.RL.7.9. CA.L.7.5a, CA.L.7.5c, CA.W.7.2a, CA.W.7.2b, CA.W.7.2c, CA.W.7.2d, CA.W.7.2f, CA.W.7.4, CA.W.7.5, CA.W.7.6, CA.W.7.9a, CA.W.7.10

Reread the poem "Elegy on the Death of Cesar Chávez." As you reread, complete the Focus Questions below. Then use your answers and annotations from the questions to help you complete the Writing Prompt.

 FOCUS QUESTIONS

1. In the first stanza of the poem, the poet uses a long simile to compare the campesinos' eyes made dry from crying over César's death with other things that the eyes could not possibly be. Highlight the comparison in the stanza and explain how it creates the desired image of something dry. Make annotations to explain how the simile works.

2. Both Rudolfo Anaya and the writers at the Cesar Chavez Foundation wrote about the life and work of César Chávez. However, the two selections, although about the same person and time period, are very different. Compare and contrast the two texts. What are the similarities between "About Cesar" and "Elegy on the Death of Cesar Chávez"? What are the differences? Focus on genre, use of language, and historical accuracy. Highlight the similarities and make annotations citing how the texts differ.

3. In lines 41-46, Anaya uses personification (giving human traits to nonhuman things) to express how he feels about the propositions. Highlight three examples of personification in the stanza. Make annotations explaining them, and tell why he might have used them to get across his point about propositions.

4. What is the denotation of the word "righteousness" in line 76 of stanza 21? What is its connotation in lines 76-79? Highlight the word and make annotations explaining your response.

5. What explicit metaphors does Anaya use in the last full stanza of the elegy, lines 98-108? Highlight these metaphors, in which one thing is said to be another. Then annotate to explain how these metaphors provide supporting evidence for the poem's message (or theme)—that Chávez dedicated his life to fighting for the human rights of migrant farm workers.

WRITING PROMPT

Think about how Rudolfo Anaya uses figurative language and connotation in "Elegy on the Death of Cesar Chavez." How does his use of figurative language and connotation help him develop his message (or theme)? Begin your writing with a clear thesis statement. Then think about what you know of Chavez from having read "About Cesar," an informational text. How do both texts support the evidence that Chavez was a protector of human rights? Use textual evidence from both texts to support Anaya's message (or theme), and draw on specific vocabulary and precise language from the selection. Consider how Anaya might have altered history a bit in his poem. Organize your support and use transitions to show the relationships among your ideas. Lastly, provide a conclusion that summarizes your main points.

HARRIET TUBMAN:

CONDUCTOR ON THE UNDERGROUND RAILROAD

NON-FICTION

Ann Petry
1955

INTRODUCTION

The years prior to the Civil War were especially perilous for escaped slaves, but Harriet Tubman returned again and again to the South to help fugitive slaves gain freedom. Where did her physical and moral courage come from? This excerpt from Ann Petry's biography of the former slave describes how 6-year-old Harriet learned about life on the plantation and came to understand the bitter

"...the patrollers were going past, in pursuit of a runaway."

 FIRST READ

NOTES

Excerpt from Chapter Three: Six Years Old

1   By the time Harriet Ross was six years old, she had **unconsciously** absorbed many kinds of knowledge, almost with the air she breathed. She could not, for example, have said how or at what moment she learned that she was a slave.

2   She knew that her brothers and sisters, her father and mother, and all the other people who lived in the quarter, men, women and children, were slaves.

3   She had been taught to say, "Yes, Missus," "No, Missus," to white women, "Yes, Mas'r," "No, Mas'r," to white men. Or, "Yes, sah," "No, sah."

4   At the same time, someone had taught her where to look for the North Star, the star that stayed **constant,** not rising in the east and setting in the west as the other stars appeared to do; and told her that anyone walking toward the North could use that star as a guide.

5   She knew about fear, too. Sometimes at night, or during the day, she heard the **furious** galloping of horses, not just one horse, several horses, thud of the hoofbeats along the road, jingle of harness. She saw the grown folks freeze into stillness, not moving, scarcely breathing, while they listened. She could not remember who first told her that those furious hoofbeats meant the patrollers were going past, in pursuit of a runaway. Only the slaves said patterollers, whispering the word.

6   Old Rit would say a prayer that the hoofbeats would not stop. If they did, there would be the dreadful sound of screams. Because the runaway slave had been caught, would be whipped, and finally sold to the chain gang.

Copyright © BookheadEd Learning, LLC

NOTES

7   Thus Harriet already shared the uneasiness and the fear of the grownups. But she shared their pleasures, too. She knew moments of pride when the overseer consulted Ben, her father, about the weather. Ben could tell if it was going to rain, when the first frost would come, tell whether there was going to be a long stretch of clear sunny days. Everyone on the plantation admired this skill of Ben's. Even the master, Edward Brodas.

8   The other slaves were in awe of Ben because he could **prophesy** about the weather. Harriet stood close to him when he studied the sky, licked his forefinger and held it up to determine the direction of the wind, then announced that there would be rain or frost or fair weather.

9   There was something free and wild in Harriet because of Ben. He talked about the arrival of the wild ducks, the thickness of the winter coat of muskrats and of rabbits. He was always talking about the woods, the berries that grew there, the strange haunting cries of some of the birds, the loud sound their wings made when they were disturbed and flew up suddenly. He spoke of the way the owls flew, their feathers so soft that they seemed to glide, soundless, through the air.

10 Ben knew about rivers and creeks and swampy places. He said that the salt water from the Bay reached into the rivers and streams for long distances. You could stick your finger in the river water and lick it and you could taste the salt from the Bay.

11 He had been all the way to the Chesapeake. He had seen storms there. He said the Big Buckwater River, which lay off to the southeast of the plantation, was just a little stream compared to the Choptank, and the Choptank was less than nothing compared to the Bay.

12 All through the plantation, from the Big House to the stables, to the fields, he had a reputation for absolute honesty. He had never been known to tell a lie. He was a valued worker and a trusted one.

13 Ben could tell wonderful stories, too. So could her mother, Old Rit, though Rit's were mostly from the Bible. Rit told about Moses and the children of Israel, about how the sea parted so that the children walked across on dry land, about the plague of locusts, about how some of the children were afraid on the long journey to the Promised Land, and so cried out: "It had been better for us to serve the Egyptians, than that we should die in the wilderness."

14 Old Rit taught Harriet the words of that song that the slaves were forbidden to sing, because of the man named Denmark Vesey, who had urged the other slaves to revolt by telling them about Moses and the children of Israel. Sometimes, in the quarter, Harriet heard snatches of it, sung under the breath,

almost whispered: "Go down, Moses. . . ." But she learned the words so well that she never forgot them.

15   She was aware of all these things and many other things too. She learned to separate the days of the week. Sunday was a special day. There was no work in the fields. The slaves cooked in the quarter and washed their clothes and sang and told stories.

16   There was another special day, issue day, which occurred at the end of the month. It was the day that food and clothes were issued to the slaves. One of the slaves was sent to the Big House, with a wagon, to bring back the monthly allowance of food. Each slave received eight pounds of pickled pork or its **equivalent** in fish, one bushel of Indian meal (corn meal), one pint of salt.

17   Once a year, on issue day, they received clothing. The men were given two tow-linen shirts, two pairs of trousers, one of tow-linen, the other woolen, and a woolen jacket for winter. The grownups received one pair of yarn stockings and a pair of shoes.

18   The children under eight had neither shoes, stockings, jacket nor trousers. They were issued two tow-linen shirts a year—short, one-piece garments made of a coarse material like burlap, reaching to the knees. These shirts were worn night and day. They were changed once a week. When they were worn out, the children went naked until the next allowance day.

19   Men and women received a coarse blanket apiece. The children kept warm as best they could.

Excerpted from *Harriet Tubman: Conductor on the Underground Railroad* by Ann Petry, published by Amistad Press.

THINK QUESTIONS
CA-CCSS: CA.RI.7.1, CA.L.7.4a, CA.L.7.4b, CA.L.7.4d, CA.SL.7.1a, CA.SL.7.1c, CA.SL.7.1d, CA.SL.7.4

1. Write two or three sentences explaining what six-year-old Harriet knew about the North Star. Support your answer with textual evidence.

2. Refer to one or more details in paragraph 5 to support your understanding of what uneasiness or fear Harriet shared with the grownups. Cite textual evidence to support your explanation.

3. Use details from paragraphs 15-18 to write two or three sentences describing which days were special to the slaves and why. Cite evidence from the text to support your explanation.

4. By remembering that the Latin prefix *un-* means "not" and the Latin suffix *-ly* means "in the manner of," use context clues to determine the meaning of the word **unconsciously** as it is used in the first paragraph of *Harriet Tubman: Conductor on the Underground Railroad*. Write your definition of "unconsciously" and tell how you determined the meaning of the word.

5. Use context to determine the meaning of the word **furious** as it is used in sentence 2 of paragraph 5 and repeated in sentence 4 of this paragraph in *Harriet Tubman: Conductor on the Underground Railroad*. Write your definition of "furious" and tell how you figured it out from the context clues. Then check the inferred meaning in the dictionary.

CLOSE READ CA-CCSS: CA.RI.7.1, CA.RI.7.3, CA.RI.7.7, CA.W.7.1a, CA.W.7.1b, CA.W.7.4, CA.W.7.5, CA.W.7.6, CA.W.7.10, CA.SL.7.2

Reread the excerpt from *Harriet Tubman: Conductor on the Underground Railroad*. As you reread, complete the Focus Questions below. Then use your answers and annotations from the questions to help you complete the Writing Prompt.

FOCUS QUESTIONS

1. What phenomenon led Tubman to realize she was a slave? How did this affect her? Cite textual evidence to support your response.

2. What was the relationship like between Harriet and her father? How do you think this relationship influenced what she went on to do with her life? Make annotations to explain your reasoning.

3. In paragraph 12, the author states that Ben "was a valued worker and a trusted one." What textual evidence in paragraphs 7–11 supports this statement? Highlight the evidence and make annotations to explain your choices.

4. What clues in the text show you that the slaves had their own language—words and phrases that they used only with each other? Make annotations citing the textual evidence of your response. What purpose do you think this special language served?

5. Harriet's father and mother both had a strong impact on her character and her life. In what ways did they influence her similarly? Are there major differences in how they impacted her? Cite specific examples from the text in your response.

WRITING PROMPT

Harriet Tubman grew up to be a defender of human rights, despite great personal risks, as demonstrated by her work on the Underground Railroad. How and why do you think she was able to achieve what she did? What drove her to take these risks? Write a short essay in which you explore Tubman's motivations and the roots of her strength of character.

Please note that excerpts and passages in the StudySync® library and this workbook are intended as touchstones to generate interest in an author's work. The excerpts and passages do not substitute for the reading of entire texts, and StudySync® strongly recommends that students seek out and purchase the whole literary or informational work in order to experience it as the author intended. Links to online resellers are available in our digital library. In addition, complete works may be ordered through an authorized reseller by filling out and returning to StudySync® the order form enclosed in this workbook.

Reading & Writing Companion **39**

THE PEOPLE COULD FLY:
AMERICAN BLACK FOLKTALES

FICTION
Virginia Hamilton
1985

INTRODUCTION

The folktales in Virginia Hamilton's book are filled with humor, magic, and mystery. In this excerpt, discover why enslaved West Africans took off their

"The young woman lifted one foot on the air. Then the other."

 FIRST READ

NOTES

1　They say the people could fly. Say that long ago in Africa, some of the people knew magic. And they would walk upon the air like climbin' up on a gate. And they flew like blackbirds over the fields. Black, shiny wings flappin' against the blue up there.

2　Then, many of the people were captured for Slavery. The ones that could fly **shed** their wings. They couldn't take their wings across the water on slave ships. Too crowded, don't you know.

3　The folks were full of **misery**, then. Got sick with the up and down of the sea. So they forgot about flyin' when they could no longer breathe the sweet scent of Africa.

4　Say the people who could fly kept their power, although they shed their wings. They looked the same as the other people from Africa who had been coming over, who had dark skin. Say you couldn't tell anymore one who could fly from one who couldn't.

5　One such who could was an old man, call him Toby. And standin' tall, yet afraid, was a young woman who once had wings. Call her Sarah. Now Sarah carried a babe tied to her back. She **trembled** to be so hard worked and scorned.

6　The slaves labored in the fields from sunup to sundown. The owner of the slaves callin' himself their Master. Say he was a hard lump of clay. A hard, glinty coal. A hard rock pile, wouldn't be moved. His Overseer on horseback pointed out the slaves who were slowin' down. So the one called Driver cracked his whip over the slow ones to make them move faster. That whip was a slice-open cut of pain. So they did move faster. Had to.

Please note that excerpts and passages in the StudySync® library and this workbook are intended as touchstones to generate interest in an author's work. The excerpts and passages do not substitute for the reading of entire texts, and StudySync® strongly recommends that students seek out and purchase the whole literary or informational work in order to experience it as the author intended. Links to online resellers are available in our digital library. In addition, complete works may be ordered through an authorized reseller by filling out and returning to StudySync® the order form enclosed in this workbook.

Reading & Writing Companion

41

NOTES

7   Sarah hoed and chopped the row as the babe on her back slept.

8   Say the child grew hungry. That babe started up **bawling** too loud. Sarah couldn't stop to feed it. Couldn't stop to soothe and quiet it down. She let it cry. She didn't want to. She had no heart to **croon** to it.

9   "Keep that thing quiet," called the Overseer. He pointed his finger at the babe. The woman scrunched low. The Driver cracked his whip across the babe anyhow. The babe hollered like any hurt child, and the woman fell to the earth.

10   The old man that was there, Toby, came and helped her to her feet.

11   "I must go soon," she told him.

12   "Soon," he said.

13   Sarah couldn't stand up straight any longer. She was too weak. The sun burned her face. The babe cried and cried, "Pity me, oh, pity me," say it sounded like. Sarah was so sad and starving, she sat down in the row.

14   "Get up, you black cow," called the Overseer. He pointed his hand and the Driver's whip snarled around Sarah's legs. Her sack dress tore into rags. Her legs bled onto the earth. She couldn't get up.

15   Toby was there where there was no one to help her and the babe.

16   "Now, before it's too late," panted Sarah. "Now, Father!"

17   "Yes, Daughter, the time is come," Toby answered. "Go as you know how to go!"

18   He raised his arms, holding them out to her. *"Kum...yali, kum buba tambe,"* and more magic words, said so quickly; they sounded like whispers and sighs.

19   The young woman lifted one foot on the air. Then the other. She flew clumsily at first, with the child now held tightly in her arms. Then she felt the magic, the African mystery. Say she rose just as free as a bird. As light as a feather.

20   The Overseer rode after her, hollerin'. Sarah flew over the fences. She flew over the woods. Tall trees could not snag her. Nor could the Overseer. She flew like an eagle now, until she was gone from sight. No one dared speak about it. Couldn't believe it. But it was, because they that was there saw that it was.

Excerpted from *The People Could Fly* by Virginia Hamilton, published by Alfred A. Knopf.

THINK QUESTIONS CA-CCSS: CA.RL.7.1, CA.RL.7.4, CA.L.7.4a, CA.L.7.4c, CA.L.7.4d

1. Why did the people lose their wings? Cite evidence from the first two paragraphs to explain your answer.

2. Why does Sarah need to leave the plantation? Use ideas that are directly stated in the text and ideas you have inferred from clues in the selection. Support your inferences with textual evidence.

3. Why is Sarah able to fly without wings at the end of the folktale? Refer to one or more details that are directly stated as well as inferences drawn from the text.

4. Use context to determine the meaning of the word **misery** as it is used in paragraph 3 of *The People Could Fly: American Black Folktales*. Write your definition of "misery" and tell how you determined its meaning. Check the inferred meaning in context, and then verify it in a print or an online dictionary.

5. By remembering that **shed** is a multiple-meaning word and that depending on its context, it may be a noun or a verb, use the context clues provided in paragraph 2 to determine the meaning of "shed" as it is used in this excerpt. Write your definition of "shed" and tell how you figured out its meaning. Consult a print or digital dictionary to determine the exact definition of the word and its part of speech, as used in the text.

Please note that excerpts and passages in the StudySync® library and this workbook are intended as touchstones to generate interest in an author's work. The excerpts and passages do not substitute for the reading of entire texts, and StudySync® strongly recommends that students seek out and purchase the whole literary or informational work in order to experience it as the author intended. Links to online resellers are available in our digital library. In addition, complete works may be ordered through an authorized reseller by filling out and returning to StudySync® the order form enclosed in this workbook.

Reading & Writing Companion   43

CLOSE READ

CA-CCSS: CA.RL.7.1, CA.RL.7.2, CA.RL.7.4, CA.RL.7.9, CA.W.7.2a, CA.W.7.2b, CA.W.7.2c, CA.W.7.2d, CA.W.7.2f, CA.W.7.4, CA.W.7.5, CA.W.7.6, CA.W.7.9a, CA.W.7.10, CA.L.7.5c

Reread the excerpt from *The People Could Fly*. As you reread, complete the Focus Questions below. Then use your answers and annotations from the questions to help you complete the Writing Prompt.

 FOCUS QUESTIONS

1. In the first paragraph of *Harriet Tubman: Conductor on the Underground Railroad*, the narrator explains that Harriet "unconsciously absorbed many kinds of knowledge, almost with the air she breathed." In paragraphs 2-4 of *The People Could Fly*, the narrator explains that the people "forgot about flyin'" when they "were captured for Slavery," yet those "who could fly kept their power." How does the idea of secret knowledge empower the slaves in both texts? Highlight textual evidence and make annotations to explain your response.

2. In paragraph 7 of *Harriet Tubman: Conductor on the Underground Railroad*, the narrator says that "Harriet already shared the uneasiness and the fear of the grownups." Based on paragraphs 5 and 6 of *Harriet Tubman* and on paragraphs 8 and 9 of *The People Could Fly*, explain how the enslaved children grew up in a culture of fear. Support your response with textual evidence and make annotations to explain your analysis.

3. In paragraph 9 of *Harriet Tubman: Conductor on the Underground Railroad*, the author describes

Ben's connection to nature by referencing a number of birds—for example, ducks and owls. In *The People Could Fly*, the narrator compares the people to blackbirds in the first paragraph and compares Sarah to an eagle in the last paragraph. Explain the connotations of these "bird" references in each text. Highlight specific evidence from the text and make annotations to explain your thinking.

4. In paragraphs 16 and 17 of *The People Could Fly*, Sarah and Toby call each other "Father" and "Daughter." Discuss the connotative meaning of these two words to explain how they express the relationship between the two characters. Highlight textual evidence and make annotations to support your response.

5. Both texts focus on the enslavement and mistreatment of African slaves during one of the most tragic periods in American history. How do the two texts demonstrate the necessity of defending human rights? Highlight textual evidence and make annotations to explain your response.

WRITING PROMPT

Harriet Tubman: Conductor on the Underground Railroad and *The People Could Fly: American Black Folktales* are similar, yet different. The first is a historical account of slavery in American history. The second is a fictional portrayal of the same topic or theme. Compare and contrast the two texts. How did Virginia Hamilton use historical fact in *The People Could Fly* to suit her purposes? Introduce your topic with a clear thesis statement. Then, organize and support your writing with specific evidence and vocabulary from both texts. Use transitions to show relationships among your ideas, and provide a conclusion that summarizes your main points.

1976 DEMOCRATIC NATIONAL CONVENTION
KEYNOTE ADDRESS

NON-FICTION
Barbara Jordan
1976

INTRODUCTION

I n 1966, Barbara Jordan became the first African-American woman elected to the Texas State Senate. She later became the first African-American woman to represent a southern state in Congress when she was elected to the U.S. House of Representatives in 1972. Jordan worked hard to improve the lives of people in her district, sponsored bills that increased workers' wages, and fought for women's rights. She was considered a gifted public speaker and, was selected to give the keynote speech at the 1976 Democratic National Convention in New York. Her highly acclaimed speech is excerpted here.

"We are a people in search of our future."

 FIRST READ

1   Thank you ladies and gentlemen for a very warm reception.

2   It was one hundred and forty-four years ago that members of the Democratic Party first met in convention to select a Presidential candidate. Since that time, Democrats have continued to convene once every four years and draft a party platform and nominate a Presidential candidate. And our meeting this week is a continuation of that tradition. But there is something different about tonight. There is something special about tonight. What is different? What is special?

3   I, Barbara Jordan, am a keynote speaker.

4   A lot of years passed since 1832, and during that time it would have been most unusual for any national political party to ask a Barbara Jordan to deliver a keynote address. But tonight, here I am. And I feel that notwithstanding the past that my presence here is one additional bit of evidence that the American Dream need not forever be **deferred.**

5   Now that I have this grand distinction, what in the world am I supposed to say? . . . I could list the many problems which Americans have. I could list the problems which cause people to feel cynical, angry, frustrated: problems which include lack of integrity in government; the feeling that the individual no longer counts; the reality of material and spiritual poverty; the feeling that the grand American experiment is failing or has failed. I could recite these problems, and then I could sit down and offer no solutions. But I don't choose to do that either. The citizens of America expect more. They deserve and they want more than a recital of problems.

6   We are a people in a **quandary** about the present. We are a people in search of our future. We are a people in search of a national community. We are a

people trying not only to solve the problems of the present, unemployment, inflation, but we are attempting on a larger scale to fulfill the promise of America. We are attempting to fulfill our national purpose, to create and sustain a society in which all of us are equal.

. . .

7   And now we must look to the future. Let us heed the voice of the people and recognize their common sense. If we do not, we not only blaspheme our political heritage, we ignore the common ties that bind all Americans. Many fear the future. Many are distrustful of their leaders, and believe that their voices are never heard. Many seek only to satisfy their private wants; to satisfy their private interests. But this is the great danger America faces—that we will cease to be one nation and become instead a collection of interest groups: city against suburb, region against region, individual against individual; each seeking to satisfy private wants. If that happens, who then will speak for America? Who then will speak for the common good?

8   This is the question which must be answered in 1976: Are we to be one people bound together by common spirit, sharing in a common **endeavor;** or will we become a divided nation? For all of its uncertainty, we cannot flee the future. We must not become the "New Puritans" and reject our society. We must address and master the future together. It can be done if we restore the belief that we share a sense of national community, that we share a common national endeavor. It can be done.

9   There is no executive order; there is no law that can require the American people to form a national community. This we must do as individuals, and if we do it as individuals, there is no President of the United States who can veto that decision.

10 As a first step, we must restore our belief in ourselves. We are a generous people, so why can't we be generous with each other? We need to take to heart the words spoken by Thomas Jefferson:

11 "Let us restore to social intercourse that harmony and that affection without which liberty and even life are but dreary things."

12 A nation is formed by the willingness of each of us to share in the responsibility for upholding the common good. A government is **invigorated** when each one of us is willing to participate in shaping the future of this nation. In this election year, we must define the "common good" and begin again to shape a common future. Let each person do his or her part. If one citizen is unwilling to participate, all of us are going to suffer. For the American idea, though it is shared by all of us, is realized in each one of us.

NOTES

13　And now, what are those of us who are elected public officials supposed to do? We call ourselves "public servants" but I'll tell you this: We as public servants must set an example for the rest of the nation. It is hypocritical for the public official to admonish and exhort the people to uphold the common good if we are derelict in upholding the common good. More is required of public officials than slogans and handshakes and press releases. More is required. We must hold ourselves strictly accountable. We must provide the people with a vision of the future.

14　If we promise as public officials, we must deliver. If we as public officials propose, we must produce. If we say to the American people, "It is time for you to be sacrificial"—sacrifice. If the public official says that, we [public officials] must be the first to give. We must be. And again, if we make mistakes, we must be willing to admit them. We have to do that. What we have to do is strike a balance between the idea that government should do everything and the idea, the belief, that government ought to do nothing. Strike a balance.

15　Let there be no **illusions** about the difficulty of forming this kind of a national community. It's tough, difficult, not easy. But a spirit of harmony will survive in America only if each of us remembers that we share a common destiny; if each of us remembers, when self-interest and bitterness seem to prevail, that we share a common destiny.

16　I have confidence that we can form this kind of national community.

• • •

17　I have that confidence.

18　We cannot improve on the system of government handed down to us by the founders of the Republic. There is no way to improve upon that. But what we can do is to find new ways to implement that system and realize our destiny.

19　Now I began this speech by commenting to you on the uniqueness of a Barbara Jordan making a keynote address. Well I am going to close my speech by quoting a Republican President and I ask you that as you listen to these words of Abraham Lincoln, relate them to the concept of a national community in which every last one of us participates:

20　"As I would not be a slave, so I would not be a master. This expresses my idea of Democracy. Whatever differs from this, to the extent of the difference, is no Democracy."

21　Thank you.

THINK QUESTIONS
CA-CCSS: CA.RI.7.1, CA.L.7.4a, CA.L.7.4d

1. Why does Barbara Jordan say in the opening to her speech that "there is something different about tonight . . . something special"? Cite one or more details from paragraph 4 to support your response.

2. What does Jordan say are some of the problems that cause the American "people to feel cynical, angry, frustrated"? Cite specific evidence from paragraph 5.

3. What does Jordan think might happen if Americans fail to "share in a common endeavor"? Cite specific evidence from paragraph 8 to explain your response.

4. Use context to determine the meaning of the word **deferred** as it is used in paragraph 4 of Jordan's keynote address to the 1976 Democratic National Convention. Write your definition of "deferred" and tell how you determined its meaning.

5. Use the context clues in paragraph 6 to determine the meaning of the word **quandary** as it is used in this keynote address. Write your definition of "quandary" and tell how you figured out its meaning. Verify your definition in a print or digital dictionary.

Please note that excerpts and passages in the StudySync® library and this workbook are intended as touchstones to generate interest in an author's work. The excerpts and passages do not substitute for the reading of entire texts, and StudySync® strongly recommends that students seek out and purchase the whole literary or informational work in order to experience it as the author intended. Links to online resellers are available in our digital library. In addition, complete works may be ordered through an authorized reseller by filling out and returning to StudySync® the order form enclosed in this workbook.

Reading & Writing Companion   **49**

CLOSE READ

CA-CCSS: CA.RI.7.1, CA.RI.7.3, CA.RI.7.6, CA.RI.7.8, CA.W.7.2a, CA.W.7.2b, CA.W.7.2c, CA.W.7.2d, CA.W.7.2e, CA.W.7.2f, CA.W.7.4, CA.W.7.5, CA.W.7.6, CA.W.7.10

Reread Barbara Jordan's speech. As you reread, complete the Focus Questions below. Then use your answers and annotations from the questions to help you complete the Writing Prompt.

FOCUS QUESTIONS

1. What does Barbara Jordan mean in paragraph 8 when she says, "We must not become the 'New Puritans' and reject our society"? What does she want the American people to do instead? Highlight textual evidence and make annotations to explain your response.

2. In paragraph 13, why does Jordan try to persuade elected public officials to "set an example" for the American people? What reasons does she give? What persuasive word does she repeat? Why? Highlight evidence in the text and make annotations to support your analysis.

3. What does Jordan mean in paragraph 15 when she says, "Let there be no illusions about the difficulty of forming this kind of a national community"? Why does she think that coming together as one nation will not be an easy task? Highlight textual evidence and make annotations to support your analysis.

4. Why do you think Jordan ends her speech with a quotation from a Republican President, Abraham Lincoln? How does the quotation support Jordan's "idea of Democracy"? Highlight textual evidence and make annotations to support your explanation.

5. In paragraph 12 of her speech, Jordan states that "[a] nation is formed by the willingness of each of us to share in the responsibility for upholding the common good." How does her view of equal participation of all citizens to uphold the "common good" illustrate that Jordan was a champion of human rights? Highlight specific evidence from the text and make annotations to support your answer.

WRITING PROMPT

How does Barbara Jordan's speech demonstrate that she believed it was essential to defend human rights? What ideas does she put forth in the speech to support this interpretation? In writing your response, use your understanding of informational text elements to analyze the interaction among individuals, ideas, and events in her speech. Begin with a clear statement to introduce your topic. Organize and support your writing with specific evidence from the text. Use precise language and selection vocabulary where possible. Develop body paragraphs and use transitions to show the relationships among your ideas. Establish a formal style that underlines the importance of your topic, and provide a conclusion that summarizes your central (or main) ideas.

THE NEW COLOSSUS

POETRY
Emma Lazarus
1883

INTRODUCTION

Emma Lazarus was a 19th century American poet best known for her work "The New Colossus," a poetic tribute to the Statue of Liberty. Originally written for a Liberty fundraiser, the poem lay forgotten for almost twenty years before revived interest led to it being engraved on a brass plaque at the base of the statue in 1903. The title of the poem refers to the Colossus of Rhodes, a towering bronze statue of the sun god Helios that was erected in the ancient Greek city of Rhodes to celebrate a military victory over Cyprus. Almost one hundred feet high, the Colossus of Rhodes was one of the tallest statues of its time and is now considered one of the Seven Wonders of the Ancient World.

"Send these, the homeless, tempest-tost to me..."

FIRST READ

1 Not like the **brazen** giant of Greek fame,
2 With conquering limbs astride from land to land;
3 Here at our sea-washed, sunset gates shall stand
4 A mighty woman with a torch, whose flame
5 Is the imprisoned lightning, and her name
6 Mother of **Exiles.** From her beacon-hand
7 Glows world-wide welcome; her mild eyes command
8 The air-bridged harbor that twin cities frame.

9 "Keep, ancient lands, your storied **pomp!**" cries she
10 With silent lips. "Give me your tired, your poor,
11 Your huddled masses yearning to breathe free,
12 The **wretched refuse** of your teeming shore.
13 Send these, the homeless, tempest-tost to me,
14 I lift my lamp beside the golden door!"

THINK QUESTIONS   CA-CCSS: CA.RL.7.1, CA.L.7.4a, CA.L.7.4c, CA.L.7.4d

1. The title of the poem refers to the Colossus of Rhodes—a giant statue of the sun god, Helios—erected in the ancient Greek city of Rhodes to celebrate the city's victory over Cyprus. How do you know from the poem that the "mighty woman with a torch" is also a statue? Cite textual evidence to support your understanding.

2. Who is the "mighty woman with a torch" not like? How is she different? Cite textual evidence to support your answer.

3. To whom is the "mighty woman with a torch" offering a "world-wide welcome"? Cite specific evidence from the poem to support your answer.

4. Use context clues and reference materials to determine two possible meanings of the word **brazen** as it is used in the first line of "The New Colossus." Write your two definitions of "brazen" and tell where you found them. Verify the part of speech and the usage for each meaning of the word.

5. Use context to determine the meaning of the word **exiles** as it is used in line 6 of "The New Colossus." Write your definition of "exiles" and tell the context clues you used to infer the meaning of the word. Then look in a print or digital dictionary to verify the meaning you inferred.

CLOSE READ
CA-CCSS: CA.RL.7.1, CA.RL.7.2, CA.RL.7.4, CA.RL.7.5, CA.L.7.5a, CA.W.7.2a, CA.W.7.2b, CA.W.7.2c, CA.W.7.2d, CA.W.7.2f, CA.W.7.4, CA.W.7.5, CA.W.7.6, CA.W.7.10

Reread the poem "The New Colossus." As you reread, complete the Focus Questions below. Then use your answers and annotations from the questions to help you complete the Writing Prompt.

FOCUS QUESTIONS

1. In line 3 of "The New Colossus," "sea-washed, sunset gates" is a metaphor. What might this metaphor mean in the context of the poem and its theme? Highlight specific evidence from the text, and make annotations recording your explanation.

2. Highlight evidence in the last six lines that "The New Colossus" is a Petrarchan sonnet. Make annotations to explain your analysis.

3. What evidence of personification can be found in lines 9–10 of the poem? Highlight specific evidence in the text, and make annotations to explain your reasoning.

4. "Tempest" is often used in a figurative sense. Highlight its use in line 13. Given the theme (or message) of the poem, how might Lazarus be using "tempest-tost" here? Make annotations recording your ideas.

5. What evidence in the last six lines supports the idea that Emma Lazarus was concerned with human rights? Highlight textual evidence and annotate to explain your reasoning.

WRITING PROMPT

Consider the use of allusion and the structure of the poem, "The New Colossus." What does Emma Lazarus want readers to know about the United States? Begin with a clear thesis statement that addresses your topic. What insight does the message (or theme) of the poem convey about the importance of defending human rights? Use your understanding of poetic structure and figurative language, particularly the allusion to the Greek Colossus that Lazarus uses in the poem, to determine her message. Organize and support your response with specific evidence from the text, including precise language and selection vocabulary wherever possible. Use transitions to show the relationships among your ideas, and provide a conclusion that summarizes your key points.

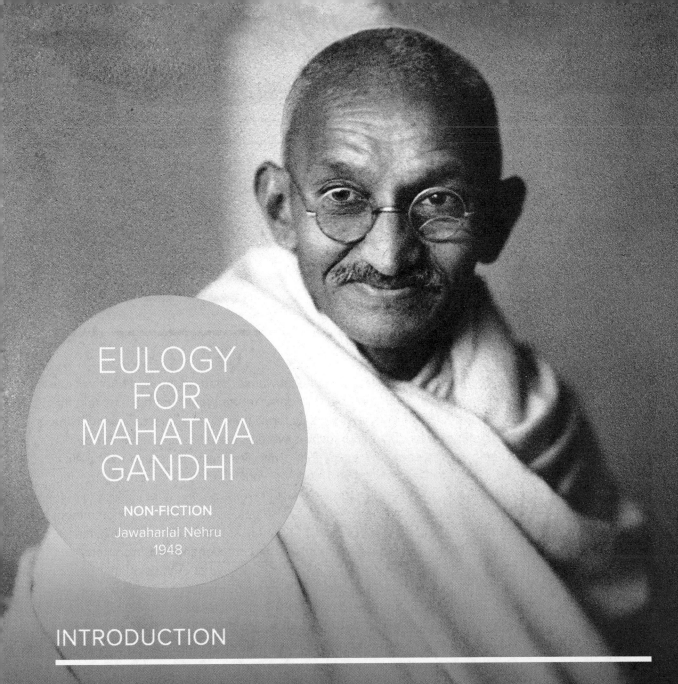

EULOGY FOR MAHATMA GANDHI

NON-FICTION
Jawaharlal Nehru
1948

INTRODUCTION

Mahatma Gandhi was born in India in 1869. At that time, India had been ruled by Great Britain for centuries. Although colonial India benefitted from mass transportation and communication systems, British rule in India was harsh. Indians endured limited rights and became economically dependent on the British colonizers. Gandhi believed that India should be free, and he worked to unite all Indians to protest British rule without using violence. Thousands of people followed Gandhi's example, and he became one of India's foremost leaders. India achieved independence in 1947, but Gandhi was assassinated the following year. Jawaharlal Nehru, a reformer who had worked side by side with Gandhi and the first prime minister after India became independent,

"He lives in the hearts of millions and he will live for immemorial ages."

FIRST READ

NOTES

1   A glory has departed and the sun that warmed and brightened our lives has set, and we shiver in the cold and dark. Yet he would not have us feel this way. After all, that glory that we saw for all these years, that man with **divine** fire, changed us also—and such as we are, we have been molded by him during these years; and out of that divine fire many of us also took a small spark which strengthened and made us work to some extent on the lines that he fashioned. And so if we praise him, our words seem rather small, and if we praise him, to some extent we also praise ourselves. Great men and **eminent** men have monuments in bronze and marble set up for them, but this man of divine fire managed in his lifetime to become **enshrined** in millions and millions of hearts so that all of us became somewhat of the stuff that he was made of, though to an infinitely lesser degree. He spread out in this way all over India, not just in palaces, or in select places or in assemblies, but in every hamlet and hut of the lowly and those who suffer. He lives in the hearts of millions and he will live for immemorial ages.

2   What, then, can we say about him except to feel humble on this occasion? To praise him we are not worthy—to praise him whom we could not follow adequately and sufficiently. It is almost doing him an injustice just to pass him by with words when he demanded work and labor and sacrifice from us; in a large measure he made this country, during the last thirty years or more, attain to heights of sacrifice which in that particular domain have never been equaled elsewhere. He succeeded in that. Yet ultimately things happened which no doubt made him suffer tremendously, though his tender face never lost its smile and he never spoke a harsh word to anyone. Yet, he must have suffered—suffered for the failing of this generation whom he had trained, suffered because we went away from the path that he had shown us. And ultimately the hand of a child of his—for he, after all, is as much a child of his as any other Indian—the hand of a child of his struck him down.

3   Long ages afterwards history will judge of this period that we have passed through. It will judge of the successes and the failures—we are too near it to be proper judges and to understand what has happened and what has not happened. All we know is that there was a glory and that it is no more; all we know is that for the moment there is darkness, not so dark certainly, because when we look into our hearts we still find the living flame which he lighted there. And if those living flames exist, there will not be darkness in this land, and we shall be able, with our effort, remembering him and following his path, to **illumine** this land again, small as we are, but still with the fire that he instilled into us.

4   He was perhaps the greatest symbol of the India of the past, and may I say, of the India of the future, that we could have had. We stand on this **perilous** edge of the present, between that past and the future to be, and we face all manner of perils. And the greatest peril is sometimes the lack of faith which comes to us, the sense of frustration that comes to us, the sinking of the heart and of the spirit that comes to us when we see ideals go overboard, when we see the great things that we talked about somehow pass into empty words, and life taking a different course. Yet, I do believe that perhaps this period will pass soon enough.

5   He has gone, and all over India there is a feeling of having been left **desolate** and forlorn. All of us sense that feeling, and I do not know when we shall be able to get rid of it. And yet together with that feeling there is also a feeling of proud thankfulness that it has been given to us of this generation to be associated with this mighty person. In ages to come, centuries and maybe millennia after us, people will think of this generation when this man of God trod on earth, and will think of us who, however small, could also follow his path and tread the holy ground where his feet had been.

6   Let us be worthy of him.

THINK QUESTIONS CA-CCSS: CA.RI.7.1, CA.L.7.4a, CA.L.7.4b, CA.L.7.4c

1. Why does Nehru feel that it is difficult to praise Gandhi? Cite evidence from paragraphs 1 and 2 to support your answer.

2. According to Nehru, what things made Gandhi suffer? Support your answer with evidence from paragraph 2.

3. Nehru states that the people of India "stand on this perilous edge of the present, between that past and the future." What perils does Nehru list? Cite textual evidence from paragraph 4 to support your response.

4. By remembering that the Greek prefix *en-* means "in," use context to determine the meaning of the word **enshrined** as it is used in the first paragraph of "Eulogy for Mahatma Gandhi." Write your definition of "enshrined" and tell the context clues you used to determine the meaning of the word.

5. Use a dictionary to look up the word **illumine** to find its origin. Notice the Latin verb from which the word comes: *illuminare*, meaning "to light up." By knowing the Latin root of the word, use the context clues provided to determine the meaning of "illumine" in paragraph 3. Write your definition of "illumine" and explain how you figured out its meaning.

CLOSE READ
CA-CCSS: CA.RI.7.1, CA.RI.7.2, CA.RI.7.3, CA.W.7.2a, CA.W.7.2b, CA.W.7.2c, CA.W.7.2d, CA.W.7.2e, CA.W.7.2f, CA.W.7.4, CA.W.7.5, CA.W.7.6, CA.W.7.10

Reread "Eulogy for Mahatma Gandhi." As you reread, complete the Focus Questions below. Then use your answers and annotations from the questions to help you complete the Writing Prompt.

 FOCUS QUESTIONS

1. When reading "Eulogy for Mahatma Gandhi," it is up to the reader to interpret Nehru's central or main ideas by making inferences from what he directly states in the text. Based on the details in the last three sentences of paragraph 1, what is the central idea that you can infer from Nehru's statements? Highlight evidence in the text and make annotations to support your explanation.

2. In paragraph 2, Nehru says, "[t]o praise him [Gandhi] we are not worthy." Find and highlight textual evidence in paragraph 2 that supports Nehru's statement. Then annotate and write a sentence summarizing the evidence.

3. Which details in paragraph 3 support Nehru's central idea that although things look dark, there is hope for the future? Highlight textual evidence and make annotations to support your choices.

4. What is the central idea of paragraph 4? Highlight the supporting details and make annotations to explain your reasoning.

5. What evidence is there in paragraphs 5 and 6 that Nehru is calling on the people of India to carry on Gandhi's fight for human rights? Highlight evidence from the text and make annotations to support your claim.

WRITING PROMPT

What are two central ideas that are developed over the course of "Eulogy for Mahatma Gandhi"? How do these two central ideas and the details that support them help to answer the Essential Question: *Why is it essential to defend human rights?* Begin with a clear thesis statement to introduce the topic. Use your understanding of the central or main idea to guide you as you identify central ideas in the selection and analyze how they relate to the Essential Question. Organize and support your writing with specific evidence from the text, including relevant selection vocabulary. Use transitions in your body paragraphs to show the relationships between (or among) your ideas. Establish a formal style to emphasize the nature of your topic, and provide a conclusion that summarizes your two central (or main) ideas.

Please note that excerpts and passages in the StudySync® library and this workbook are intended as touchstones to generate interest in an author's work. The excerpts and passages do not substitute for the reading of entire texts, and StudySync® strongly recommends that students seek out and purchase the whole literary or informational work in order to experience it as the author intended. Links to online resellers are available in our digital library. In addition, complete works may be ordered through an authorized reseller by filling out and returning to StudySync® the order form enclosed in this workbook.

Reading & Writing Companion   **59**

LONG WALK TO FREEDOM

NON-FICTION
Nelson Mandela
1994

INTRODUCTION

studysync tv

From prisoner to president of South Africa, Nelson Mandela was one of the political stories of the twentieth century. In 1944, Mandela became a leader in the African National Congress, a political party that opposed South Africa's policy of racial segregation. In 1962, Mandela was jailed for his political activities, and after a widely publicized trial, was sentenced to life in prison. Over the years, Mandela became the world's best-known political prisoner, gaining international support for his fight against apartheid. He was released from captivity in 1990, and went on to become South Africa's first black president. The excerpt here is from

"Man's goodness is a flame that can be hidden but never extinguished."

FIRST READ

NOTES

From Part Eleven: Freedom

1   On the day of the inauguration, I was overwhelmed with a sense of history. In the first decade of the twentieth century, a few years after the bitter Anglo-Boer War and before my own birth, the white-skinned peoples of South Africa patched up their differences and erected a system of racial domination against dark-skinned peoples of their own land. The structure they created formed the basis of one of the harshest, most inhumane societies the world has ever known. Now, in the last decade of the twentieth century, and my own eighth decade as a man, that system had been overturned forever and replaced by one that recognized the rights and freedoms of all peoples regardless of the color of their skin.

2   That day had come about through the unimaginable sacrifices of thousands of my people, people whose suffering and courage can never be counted or repaid. I felt that day, as I have on so many other days, that I was simply the sum of all those African patriots who had gone before me. That long and noble line ended and now began again with me. I was pained that I was not able to thank them and that they were not able to see what their sacrifices had wrought.

3   The policy of **apartheid** created a deep and lasting wound in my country and my people. All of us will spend many years, if not generations, recovering from that profound hurt. But the decades of oppression and **brutality** had another, unintended effect, and that was that it produced the Oliver Tambos, the Walter Sisulus, the Chief Luthulis, the Yusuf Dadoos, the Bram Fischers, the Robert Sobukwes of our time—men of such extraordinary courage, wisdom, and generosity that their like may never be known again. Perhaps it requires such depth of **oppression** to create such heights of character. My country is rich in the minerals and gems that lie beneath its soil, but I have

Please note that excerpts and passages in the StudySync® library and this workbook are intended as touchstones to generate interest in an author's work. The excerpts and passages do not substitute for the reading of entire texts, and StudySync® strongly recommends that students seek out and purchase the whole literary or informational work in order to experience it as the author intended. Links to online resellers are available in our digital library. In addition, complete works may be ordered through an authorized reseller by filling out and returning to StudySync® the order form enclosed in this workbook.

Reading & Writing Companion   **61**

always known that its greatest wealth is its people, finer and truer than the purest diamonds.

4   It is from these comrades in the struggle that I learned the meaning of courage. Time and again, I have seen men and women risk and give their lives for an idea. I have seen men stand up to attacks and torture without breaking, showing a strength and **resiliency** that defies the imagination. I learned that courage was not the absence of fear, but the triumph over it. I felt fear myself more times than I can remember, but I hid it behind a mask of boldness. The brave man is not he who does not feel afraid, but he who conquers that fear.

5   I never lost hope that this great **transformation** would occur. Not only because of the great heroes I have already cited, but because of the courage of the ordinary men and women of my country. I always knew that deep down in every human heart, there is mercy and generosity. No one is born hating another person because of the color of his skin, or his background, or his religion. People must learn to hate, and if they can learn to hate, they can be taught to love, for love comes more naturally to the human heart than its opposite. Even in the grimmest times in prison, when my comrades and I were pushed to our limits, I would see a glimmer of humanity in one of the guards, perhaps just for a second, but it was enough to reassure me and keep me going. Man's goodness is a flame that can be hidden but never extinguished.

6   We took up the struggle with our eyes wide open, under no illusion that the path would be an easy one. As a young man, when I joined the African National Congress, I saw the price my comrades paid for their beliefs, and it was high. For myself, I have never regretted my commitment to the struggle, and I was always prepared to face the hardships that affected me personally. But my family paid a terrible price, perhaps too dear a price for my commitment.

7   In life, every man has twin obligations—obligations to his family, to his parents, to his wife and children; and he as an obligation to his people, his community, his country. In a civil and human society, each man is able to fulfill those obligations according to his own inclinations and abilities. But in a country like South Africa, it was almost impossible for a man of my birth and color to fulfill both of those obligations. In South Africa, a man of color who attempted to live as a human being was punished and isolated. In South Africa, a man who tried to fulfill his duty to his people was inevitably ripped from his family and home and was forced to live a life apart, a twilight existence of secrecy and rebellion. I did not in the beginning choose to place my people above my family, but in attempting to serve my people, I found that I was prevented from serving my obligations as a son, a brother, a father, and a husband.

Copyright © BookheadEd Learning, LLC

8   In that way, my commitment to my people, to the millions of South Africans I would never know or meet, was at the expense of the people I knew best and loved most. It was as simple and yet as incomprehensible as the moment a small child asks her father, "Why can you not be with us?" And the father must utter the terrible words: "There are other children like you, a great many of them. . . " and then one's voice trails off.

9   I was not born with a hunger to be free. I was born free—free in every way that I could know. Free to run in the fields near my mother's hut, free to swim in the clear stream that ran through my village, free to roast mealies under the stars and ride the broad backs of slow-moving bulls. As long as I obeyed my father and abided by the customs of my tribe, I was not troubled by the laws of man or God.

10   It was only when I began to learn that my boyhood freedom was an illusion, when I discovered as a young man that my freedom had already been taken from me, that I began to hunger for it. At first, as a student, I wanted freedom only for myself, the transitory freedoms of being able to stay out at night, read what I pleased, and go where I chose. Later, as a young man in Johannesburg, I yearned for the basic and honorable freedoms of achieving my potential, of earning my keep, of marrying and having a family—the freedom not to be obstructed in a lawful life.

11   But then I slowly saw that not only was I not free, but my brothers and sisters were not free. I saw that it was not just my freedom that was curtailed, but the freedom of everyone who looked like I did. That is when I joined the African National Congress, and that is when the hunger for my own freedom became the greater hunger for the freedom of my people to live their lives with dignity and self-respect that animated my life, that transformed a frightened young man into a bold one, that drove a law-abiding attorney to become a criminal, that turned a family-loving husband into a man without a home, that forced a life-loving man to live like a monk. I am not more virtuous or self-sacrificing than the next man, but I found that I could not even enjoy the poor and limited freedoms I was allowed when I knew my people were not free. Freedom is indivisible; the chains on any one of my people were the chains on all of them, the chains on all of my people were the chains on me.

12   It was during those long and lonely years that my hunger for the freedom of my own people became a hunger for the freedom of all people, white and black. I knew as well as I knew anything that the oppressor must be liberated just as surely as the oppressed. A man who takes away another man's freedom is a prisoner of hatred, he is locked behind the bars of prejudice and narrow-mindedness. I am not truly free if I am taking away someone else's freedom, just as surely as I am not free when my freedom is taken from me. The oppressed and the oppressor alike are robbed of their humanity.

Reading & Writing
Companion

13   When I walked out of prison, that was my mission, to liberate the oppressed and the oppressor both. Some say that has now been achieved. But I know that is not the case. The truth is that we are not yet free; we have merely achieved the freedom to be free, the right not to be oppressed. We have not taken the final step of our journey, but the first step on a longer and even more difficult road. For to be free is not merely to cast off one's chains, but to live in a way that respects and enhances the freedom of others. The true test of our devotion to freedom is just beginning.

14   I walked that long road to freedom. I have tried not to falter; I have made missteps along the way. But I have discovered the secret that after climbing a great hill, one only finds that there are many more hills to climb. I have taken a moment here to rest, to steal a view of the glorious vista that surrounds me, to look back on the distance I have come. But I can rest only for a moment, for with freedom comes responsibility, and I dare not linger, for my long walk is not yet ended.

From *Long Walk to Freedom* by Nelson Mandela. Copyright © 1994, 1995 by Nelson Rolihlahla Mandela. Reprinted by permission of Little, Brown and Company.

THINK QUESTIONS CA-CCSS: CA.RI.7.1, CA.RI.7.4, CA.L.7.4a, CA.L.7.4b, CA.SL.7.1a, CA.SL.7.1b, CA.SL.7.1c, CA.SL.7.1d, CA.SL.7.2

1. Use details from the first paragraph to explain the social and political changes that have taken place in South Africa since the 1990s.

2. Write two or three sentences explaining Mandela's point of view about courage and his own reaction to fear. Support your answer with evidence from paragraph 4.

3. Refer to one or more details to explain Mandela's view of a person's "twin obligations"—both from ideas that are directly stated in paragraph 7 and from ideas you have inferred from clues in the text.

4. Use context clues and word relationships to determine the meaning of the word **resiliency** as it is used in paragraph 4 of *Long Walk to Freedom*. Write your definition of "resiliency" here and tell how you determined its meaning.

5. By recalling that the Latin prefix *trans-* means "across" or "to change completely" and that the suffix *-ation* means "act or process," use the context clues provided in paragraph 5 to determine the meaning of **transformation**. Write your definition of "transformation" and tell how you figured out its meaning.

CLOSE READ CA-CCSS: CA.RI.7.1, CA.RI.7.3, CA.RI.7.6, CA.RI.7.5, CA.W.7.2

Reread the excerpt from *Long Walk to Freedom*. As you reread, complete the Focus Questions below. Then use your answers and annotations from the questions to help you complete the Writing Prompt.

 FOCUS QUESTIONS

1. Based on paragraph 3, explain Mandela's point of view regarding the effects of apartheid on South Africa and its people. Highlight evidence from the text and make annotations to explain your response.

2. In paragraph 5, analyze Mandela's point of view regarding the qualities of a courageous person and a person who lacks courage. To which category does Mandela belong? To which category does the guard belong? Support your answer with textual evidence and inferences. Make annotations justifying your response.

3. Based on paragraph 10, explain Mandela's point of view regarding "transitory freedoms" and

"basic and honorable freedoms." Highlight textual evidence and make annotations to support your explanation.

4. In paragraph 13, what does Mandela want the reader to know about freedom? What action does he want people to take? Highlight your evidence and make annotations to support your explanation.

5. How might Mandela respond to the Essential Question: *Why is it essential to defend human rights?* Highlight textual evidence and make annotations to explain your ideas.

WRITING PROMPT

This excerpt from Nelson Mandela's autobiography *Long Walk to Freedom* may be more philosophical than autobiographical as he reflects on oppression and transformation in South Africa. How does Mandela influence people's views about courage and freedom through his observations about and experiences with apartheid? In what ways do Mandela's observations and experiences impact his own feelings about the importance of defending human rights? Use your understanding of author's purpose and point of view in your response. Support your writing with strong reasons and specific evidence from the text.

Please note that excerpts and passages in the StudySync® library and this workbook are intended as touchstones to generate interest in an author's work. The excerpts and passages do not substitute for the reading of entire texts, and StudySync® strongly recommends that students seek out and purchase the whole literary or informational work in order to experience it as the author intended. Links to online resellers are available in our digital library. In addition, complete works may be ordered through an authorized reseller by filling out and returning to StudySync® the order form enclosed in this workbook.

Reading & Writing Companion   **65**

TAKING A STAND

English Language
Development

NON-FICTION

INTRODUCTION

Bullying is a widespread problem, and it can happen anywhere—in school, during activities, or online. This article, "Taking a Stand," details seventh-grader Isabella Petrini's decision to speak out against bullying. Once a bully herself, Petrini started an anti-bullying program at her school. Through it she convinced many others to stop being mean and start trying to understand

"In 2014, about 30 percent of students reported having been bullied at school or online."

FIRST READ

NOTES

1 Imagine your worst day at school. It wasn't about failing a test. Maybe you got to class and heard muffled giggling. Maybe you heard buzzing whispers behind you in the hall. Maybe later at home you wept blinding tears.

2 Students often worry about doing well in school. But for many, there's something more worrisome: **bullying**. Bullying is "unwanted, **aggressive** behavior." It is inflicted on someone considered weak or vulnerable. It can happen face to face or through **digital platforms** such as texting and social media.

3 Bullying hurts many students. In 2014, about 30 percent of students reported having been bullied at school or online. Many don't report bullying. More than 60 percent choose to remain quiet. They endure the sickening fear and feel helpless.

4 Bullying has costs. Bullied students are more likely to have health problems like depression and anxiety. They are more likely to struggle in school. Some become bullies themselves.

5 Isabella Petrini knows about bullying. In fifth grade, she was a bully. She and her friends would say cruel things about other students. But by the time she reached seventh grade, Petrini saw bullying differently. She realized that these remarks weren't harmless talk among friends. They were biting comments with potential for harm.

6 When Petrini saw the television program *If You Really Knew Me,* she had an idea. On the program, real-life high school students come together and talk about bullying. The program's goal is to help stop bullying by helping people understand one another.

7 The program turned Petrini into an activist. She wanted to begin an anti-bullying initiative at her own school. She and her friends agreed that the

Please note that excerpts and passages in the StudySync® library and this workbook are intended as touchstones to generate interest in an author's work. The excerpts and passages do not substitute for the reading of entire texts, and StudySync® strongly recommends that students seek out and purchase the whole literary or informational work in order to experience it as the author intended. Links to online resellers are available in our digital library. In addition, complete works may be ordered through an authorized reseller by filling out and returning to StudySync® the order form enclosed in this workbook.

Reading & Writing Companion **67**

school could be a better place. People needed to accept one another instead of making stinging insults or passing silent judgement. As Petrini told a reporter, "We just realized, it's like you're an iceberg. Ninety percent of you is what you really are, under the surface. Only 10 percent of you is your image, what other people see. A lot of people are judged on the way that they look. And we didn't think that was fair."

8 The girls made plans. First they presented their idea to the principal. He gave it full support. Petrini and her friends then organized a school-wide assembly. Petrini showed part of *If You Really Knew Me.* The audience watched with wide-eyed attention. Students were asked to sign a **pledge** against bullying. The program became popular. Students liked that it was started by their peers.

9 Petrini and her friends continued their fight. They joined with others in school. Together, they came up with ideas such as no-bullying zones. They continued to focus on understanding others and standing up to bullying.

⚙ USING LANGUAGE CA-CCSS: ELD.PII.7.4.Ex

Complete the sentences below by filling in the blank or blanks.

1. **Complete the sentence with the appropriate noun(s). Use information from paragraph 2.**

   _____ is aggressive or unwanted behavior.

2. **Complete the sentence with the appropriate noun(s). Use information from paragraph 4.**

   Bullied students are more likely to have health problems like _____ and

   _____.

3. **Complete the sentence with the appropriate noun(s). Use information from paragraph 5.**

   Petrini realized that mean _____ weren't jokes.

4. **Complete the sentence with the appropriate noun(s). Use information from paragraph 7.**

   Petrini became an _____ and began an anti-bullying _____

   at her _____.

5. **Complete the sentence with the appropriate noun(s). Use information from paragraph 8.**

   Petrini asked other _____ to sign a _____.

MEANINGFUL INTERACTIONS CA-CCSS: ELD.PI.7.1.Ex, ELD.PI.7.10.b.Ex

Work with your partner or group to identify main ideas and details in "Taking a Stand" and complete the sentences. Then, on a separate piece of paper, use this information to write a brief summary in your own words. Use the self-assessment rubric to evaluate your participation in the activity.

2 Bullying is "_____, _____." It is inflicted on someone considered _____. It can happen _____, or through _____.

4 Bullying has _____. Bullied students are more likely to have _____ like _____ and _____. They are more likely to _____.

5 Isabella Petrini knows _____. She and her friends would _____ _____. But by the time she _____. Petrini _____ differently. She realized that _____ among friends. They were_____ with _____.

7 She wanted to begin an _____. She and her friends agreed that _____. People needed to _____ instead of _____ or _____.

9 Petrini and her friends continued _____. They _____ _____. Together, they _____ such as _____. They continued to focus on _____ and _____.

SELF-ASSESSMENT RUBRIC CA-CCSS: ELD.PI.7.1.Ex , ELD.PI.7.10.b.Ex

	4 I did this well.	3 I did this pretty well.	2 I did this a little bit.	1 I did not do this.
I took an active part with others in doing the activity.				
I contributed effectively to the group's decisions.				
I understood the presentation of main ideas and some details in the selection.				
I helped others understand the main ideas and some details in the selection.				
I completed the sentences carefully and accurately.				

Please note that excerpts and passages in the StudySync® library and this workbook are intended as touchstones to generate interest in an author's work. The excerpts and passages do not substitute for the reading of entire texts, and StudySync® strongly recommends that students seek out and purchase the whole literary or informational work in order to experience it as the author intended. Links to online resellers are available in our digital library. In addition, complete works may be ordered through an authorized reseller by filling out and returning to StudySync® the order form enclosed in this workbook.

Reading & Writing Companion

69

REREAD

Reread "Taking a Stand." After you reread, complete the Using Language and Meaningful Interactions activities.

⚙ USING LANGUAGE CA-CCSS: ELD.PII.7.4.Ex

Read "Taking a Stand" carefully to find the nouns listed below and the adjectives that describe them. Complete the center column of the chart by providing the adjective that describes each noun listed in the Noun column. Then complete the Sense column by naming the sense to which the adjective refers. If the adjective is not a sensory adjective, write "none." The first two rows have been completed for you.

Noun	Adjective	Sense
day	worst	none
giggling	muffled	hearing
whispers		
tears		
behavior		
students		
initiative		
fear		
place		
insults		
judgment		
attention		

MEANINGFUL INTERACTIONS CA-CCSS: ELD.PI.7.1.Ex, ELD.PI.7.11.a.Ex

Given what you have read in "Taking a Stand," what do you think of Isabella Petrini's actions in fifth and seventh grade? Do you think her initiative will be successful? Work in small groups to practice sharing and discussing your opinions, using the speaking frames. Then use the self-assessment rubric to evaluate your participation in the discussion.

- I think Isabella used to be . . . because . . .

- I think she became . . . because she . . .

- Do you think . . . ?

- Why do you think . . . ?

- I think you said . . .

- I think her . . . because . . .

- I agree / don't agree . . .

 SELF-ASSESSMENT RUBRIC CA-CCSS: ELD.PI.7.1.Ex, ELD.PI.7.11.a.Ex

	4 I did this well.	3 I did this pretty well.	2 I did this a little bit.	1 I did not do this.
I expressed my opinion clearly.				
I listened carefully to others' opinions and gave everyone a chance to share.				
I built on the opinions of my group members.				
I was courteous when persuading others to share my view.				

REREAD

Reread "Taking a Stand." After you reread, complete the Using Language and Meaningful Interactions activities.

USING LANGUAGE   CA-CCSS: ELD.PII.7.5.Ex

Read the excerpts from "Taking a Stand" listed in the first column. Complete the second column by expanding the sentence to include the prepositional phrase that tells where each excerpt takes place. Base your choices on locations mentioned in "Taking a Stand." The first one has been done for you.

Excerpt	Prepositional Phrase Describing Location
Imagine your worst day . . .	at school
Maybe you got . . .	
Maybe you heard buzzing whispers . . .	
Maybe later . . . you wept blinding tears.	
Bullying can happen . . . such as texting and social media.	
Bullied students are more likely to struggle . . .	
Petrini wanted to begin an anti-bullying initiative . . .	
Ninety percent of you is what you really are, . . .	

Reading & Writing Companion

MEANINGFUL INTERACTIONS CA-CCSS: ELD.PI.7.1.Ex, ELD.PI.7.3.Ex, ELD.PI.7.11.a.Ex

Do you think that Isabella Petrini will succeed with her initiative? What evidence from the text supports your opinion? With a partner, use the speaking frames to prepare your presentation. Before presenting, take turns practicing with your partner. Make suggestions and ask each other questions to clarify opinions, to be sure you understand what your partner is saying, and to verify evidence. You may refer to to earlier group discussions and notes while practicing or presenting.

- My opinion is that Isabella Petrini will / will not . . . because . . .

- My opinion is based on . . .

- This evidence supports the idea that . . .

- I think you said that . . .

- Yes, I see your opinion is based on evidence in paragraph . . .

- Perhaps you could add more text evidence, such as . . .

- Do you have background knowledge to add?

- If so, you could add . . .

A LONG FIGHT FOR DEMOCRACY

English Language
Development

NON-FICTION

INTRODUCTION

When Aung San Suu Kyi returned to her native country, Myanmar, in 1988, she found it in a state of crisis. The people there were fighting against a brutal dictator. They faced hardships—and even death—for their protests. What she saw inspired Suu Kyi to begin a decades-long fight for democracy in Myanmar. She knew that the fight would not be easy and that she would face untold challenges along the way. But to this day, she hasn't given up

"Fear is a habit; I am not afraid."
-Aung San Suu Kyi

 FIRST READ

1   From childhood, Aung San Suu Kyi has lived in a world of politics, struggles, and fights for justice. Suu Kyi was born June 19, 1945, in Rangoon, Burma. Her father was a hero in Burma's fight for independence. He was assassinated when Suu Kyi was only two. Suu Kyi's mother was an ambassador to India in the 1960s. Suu Kyi lived in India with her mother. She **witnessed** the effects of Mahatma Gandhi's earlier fight for India's independence.

2   Suu Kyi did not return to Burma after finishing her education in India. She studied at Oxford University in England. She then lived and worked for many years in England, the United States, and India.

3   In 1988, Suu Kyi decided to return to Burma. She wanted to care for her mother, who lived there then. This decision **transformed** Suu Kyi's life.

4   Suu Kyi was shocked by what she saw in her homeland. Burma was in **crisis**. Burma's military had **seized** power. The residents of Burma were **protesting** the new government. Many were killed. In a speech that year, Suu Kyi said, "I could not as my father's daughter remain **indifferent** to all that was going on." At that moment, Suu Kyi established her long fight for democracy in Burma. Burma later was renamed Myanmar.

5   During her fight for democracy in her country, Suu Kyi had many accomplishments. She had many setbacks too. Her ups and downs included the following events:

- Recognition of her work for democracy. The people of Myanmar saw that Suu Kyi could change things.
- House arrest by Burma's military government beginning in 1989.

Please note that excerpts and passages in the StudySync® library and this workbook are intended as touchstones to generate interest in an author's work. The excerpts and passages do not substitute for the reading of entire texts, and StudySync® strongly recommends that students seek out and purchase the whole literary or informational work in order to experience it as the author intended. Links to online resellers are available in our digital library. In addition, complete works may be ordered through an authorized reseller by filling out and returning to StudySync® the order form enclosed in this workbook.

Reading & Writing Companion   **75**

- Victory for her political party, the National League for Democracy (NLD), in 1990. The people of Myanmar elected the NLD. However, the military government ignored the results of this election.
- Release from house arrest after the 1990 election.
- Receipt of the Nobel Peace Prize in 1991. The Nobel Committee recognized Suu Kyi's work for democracy.
- Formation of a democratic committee in 1998. Suu Kyi proclaimed this committee the official government of Myanmar. The military government put her under house arrest again. It did not recognize the committee, but the world took notice.
- Receipt of the Congressional Gold Medal in 2007. The U.S. Congress gave Suu Kyi this important award. She was the first person to receive the award while in prison.
- Election to Myanmar's parliament in 2012. Suu Kyi was elected easily. She has served in parliament since that time.

6   Though Suu Kyi has accomplished much, her fight has been difficult. Suu Kyi is continuing to fight for the rights of the people of Myanmar. She fights without fear. "Fear is a habit; I am not afraid," said Suu Kyi.

USING LANGUAGE CA-CCSS: ELD.PII.7.3.Ex, ELD.PII.7.3.Br

Write the correct verb or verb phrase in each blank.

1. Write the correct **past** tense of the verb "be" in the following sentence:

   Aung San Suu Kyi's father _____ a hero in Burma's fight for independence.

2. Write the correct **past** tense of the verbs "live" and "work" in the following sentence:

   Suu Kyi _____ and _____ in England, the United States, and India.

3. Write the correct **past** tense of the verb "transform" in the following sentence:

   Suu Kyi's decision to return to Burma _____ her life.

4. Write the correct **past perfect** tense of the verb "seize" in the following sentence:

   When Suu Kyi arrived in Burma, the military _____ control of the government.

5. Write the correct **past progressive** tense of the verb "protest" in the following sentence:

   The residents of Burma _____ against the military.

6. Write the correct **past** tense of the verb "put" in the following sentence:

   The military government _____ Suu Kyi under house arrest more than one time.

7. Write the correct **past** tense of the verb "recognize" in the following sentence:

   The Nobel Committee _____ Suu Kyi's work for democracy.

8. Write the correct **present perfect** tense of the verb "serve" in the following sentence:

   Suu Kyi _____ in the Myanmar parliament since 2012.

Please note that excerpts and passages in the StudySync® library and this workbook are intended as touchstones to generate interest in an author's work. The excerpts and passages do not substitute for the reading of entire texts, and StudySync® strongly recommends that students seek out and purchase the whole literary or informational work in order to experience it as the author intended. Links to online resellers are available in our digital library. In addition, complete works may be ordered through an authorized reseller by filling out and returning to StudySync® the order form enclosed in this workbook.

Reading & Writing
Companion

77

👥 MEANINGFUL INTERACTIONS CA-CCSS: ELD.PI.7.1.Ex, ELD.PI.7.6.b.Ex

Work with your partner or group to express conclusions based on information in "A Long Fight for Democracy" and complete the writing frames below. Then use the self-assessment rubric to evaluate your participation in the discussion.

In paragraph 1, the author writes, "Her father was a hero in Burma's fight for independence. He was assassinated when Suu Kyi was only two."

- One conclusion I can express based on this information is that Suu Kyi's father_____

_____.

In paragraph 1, the author writes, "She witnessed the effects of Mahatma Gandhi's earlier fight for India's independence."

- One conclusion I can express based on this information is that what Suu Kyi saw in India _____

_____.

In paragraph 4, the author writes, "Suu Kyi was shocked by what she saw in her homeland. Burma was in crisis. Burma's military had seized power."

- One conclusion I can express based on this information is that the military's seizing power was _____

_____.

Keep the discussion moving forward by affirming one another and adding to each other's ideas using the speaking frames below.

- I think . . . made a good point when they said . . .
- . . . , that's a great start, let me build on that by adding . . .
- Another example that supports this conclusion is . . .

⊟ SELF-ASSESSMENT RUBRIC CA-CCSS: ELD.PI.7.1.Ex, ELD.PI.7.6.b.Ex

	4 I did this well.	3 I did this pretty well.	2 I did this a little bit.	1 I did not do this.
I took an active part with others in doing the assigned task.				
I kept a positive attitude and made an effort to affirm the other members of my group.				
I contributed to the group's discussion by adding relevant information and evidence.				
I completed the sentence frames for expressing conclusions carefully and accurately.				

REREAD

Reread "A Long Fight for Democracy." After you reread, complete the Using Language and Meaningful Interactions activities.

USING LANGUAGE   CA-CCSS: ELD.PII.7.2.a.Ex

Read each passage from "A Long Fight for Democracy." Think about the words in bold. Then choose the answer which the words refer to.

1. Suu Kyi lived in India with her mother. **She** witnessed the effects of Mahatma Gandhi's earlier fight for India's independence.

    ○ Suu Kyi
    ○ Suu Kyi's mother

2. In 1988, Suu Kyi decided to return to Burma. She wanted to care for her mother, **who** lived there then.

    ○ Suu Kyi
    ○ Suu Kyi's mother

3. Burma was in crisis. Burma's military had seized power. The residents of Burma were protesting the new government. **Many** were killed.

    ○ members of Burma's military
    ○ residents of Burma

4. In a speech that year, Suu Kyi said, "I could not as my **father's daughter** remain indifferent to all that was going on."

    ○ Suu Kyi
    ○ Suu Kyi's father

5. Suu Kyi proclaimed this committee the official government of Myanmar. The military government put **her** under house arrest again.

    ○ Suu Kyi
    ○ the military government

6. Receipt of the Congressional Gold Medal in 2007. The U.S. Congress gave Suu Kyi **this impressive award**. She was the first person to receive **the award** while imprisoned.

    ○ the Congressional Gold Medal
    ○ the U.S. Congress

MEANINGFUL INTERACTIONS CA-CCSS: ELD.PI.7.4.Ex, ELD.PI.7.6.a.Ex

Throughout her life, Aung San Suu Kyi has had many accomplishments and experienced many setbacks. Both her accomplishments and setbacks have causes. Consider the cause-and-effect relationships the author explains in "A Long Fight for Democracy." Work with a partner or in a small group to practice identifying and discussing cause-and-effect relationships, using the speaking frames. Then use the self-assessment rubric to evaluate your participation in the discussion.

- Suu Kyi returns to Burma and sees that the country is in crisis. This is a . . .

- The effect is . . .

- Suu Kyi begins to work for democracy. This is a . . .

- The effect is . . .

- The Nobel Committee recognized Suu Kyi's work for democracy. This is a . . .

- The effect is . . .

SELF-ASSESSMENT RUBRIC CA-CCSS: ELD.PI.7.4.Ex, ELD.PI.7.6.a.Ex

	4 I did this well.	3 I did this pretty well.	2 I did this a little bit.	1 I did not do this.
I discussed cause-and-effect relationships clearly.				
I listened carefully to others' ideas.				
I spoke respectfully when disagreeing with ideas.				
I used details from the text when discussing cause-and-effect relationships.				

REREAD

Reread "A Long Fight for Democracy." After you reread, complete the Using Language and Meaningful Interactions activities.

USING LANGUAGE CA-CCSS: ELD.PII.7.5.Ex

Complete the chart by using prepositional phrases to add detail to sentences. For each item, look at the purpose for modifying to add detail. Using the prepositional phrases from the word box, choose a phrase that best completes the sentence and enter it into the last column.

Prepositional Phrase Options		
at Oxford University; in India	without fear	in crisis
during her fight	in Rangoon, Burma	in 2012; since that time

Purpose for Modifying to Add Detail	Sentence	Prepositional Phrase or Phrases
to tell where	Aung San Suu Kyi was born June 19, 1945, _____.	
to tell where	Suu Kyi studied _____ after finishing her education _____.	
to tell when	Suu Kyi was elected to Myanmar's parliament _____ and has served in parliament _____.	
to tell how	When Suu Kyi returned to Burma, the country was _____.	
to tell when	Suu Kyi had many accomplishments _____ for democracy.	
to tell how	Suu Kyi fights for people's rights _____.	

Copyright © BookheadEd Learning, LLC

MEANINGFUL INTERACTIONS   CA-CCSS: ELD.PI.7.6.a.Ex, ELD.PI.7.9.Ex

In the previous lesson, you identified and discussed cause-and-effect relationships the author presents in "A Long Fight for Democracy." Which cause-and-effect relationship do you think is most important in the life of Aung San Suu Kyi? Work with your partner or small group to share and discuss your ideas. Then, use the writing frames below to record your thoughts. Be prepared to present your ideas to the class.

- An important cause-and-effect relationship in Suu Kyi's life is _____
_____.

- In this cause-and-effect relationship, the cause is _____, and the effect is
_____.

- This cause-and-effect relationship is important because _____
_____.

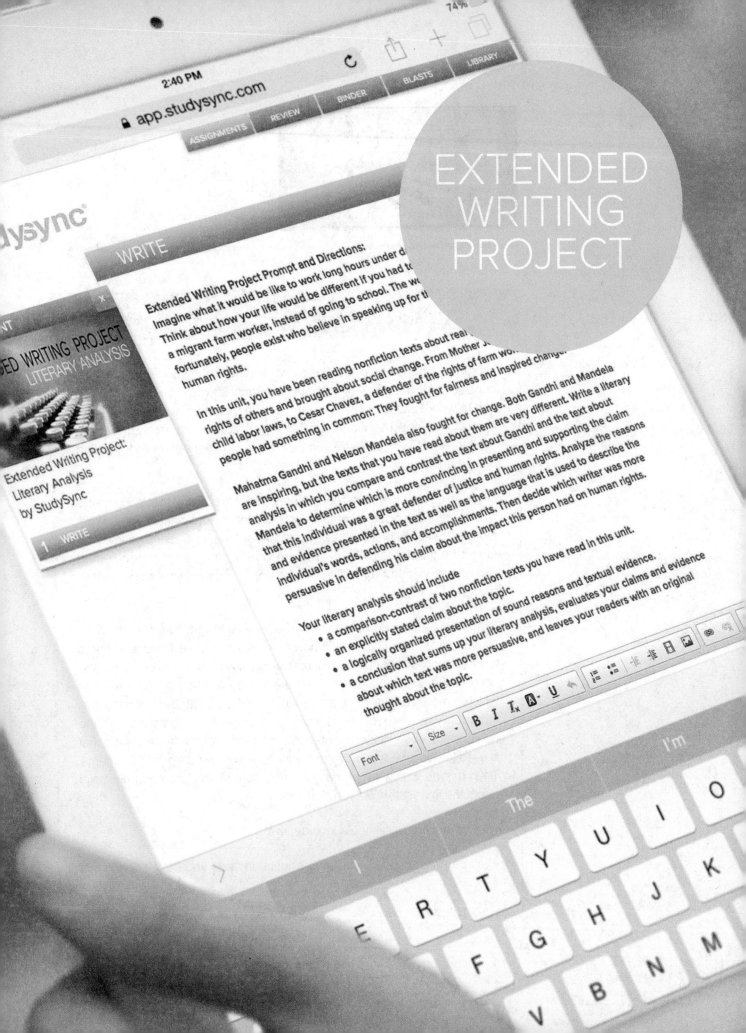

EXTENDED WRITING PROJECT

app.studysync.com

2:40 PM   74%

ASSIGNMENTS   REVIEW   BINDER   BLASTS   LIBRARY

WRITE

dysync

EXTENDED WRITING PROJECT
LITERARY ANALYSIS

Extended Writing Project:
Literary Analysis
by StudySync

1   WRITE

Extended Writing Project Prompt and Directions:

Imagine what it would be like to work long hours under da...
Think about how your life would be different if you had to...
a migrant farm worker, instead of going to school. The wo...
fortunately, people exist who believe in speaking up for th...
human rights.

In this unit, you have been reading nonfiction texts about real ...
rights of others and brought about social change. From Mother J...
child labor laws, to Cesar Chavez, a defender of the rights of farm wo...
people had something in common: They fought for fairness and inspired change...

Mahatma Gandhi and Nelson Mandela also fought for change. Both Gandhi and Mandela
are inspiring, but the texts that you have read about them are very different. Write a literary
analysis in which you compare and contrast the text about Gandhi and the text about
Mandela to determine which is more convincing in presenting and supporting the claim
that this individual was a great defender of justice and human rights. Analyze the reasons
and evidence presented in the text as well as the language that is used to describe the
individual's words, actions, and accomplishments. Then decide which writer was more
persuasive in defending his claim about the impact this person had on human rights.

Your literary analysis should include
• a comparison-contrast of two nonfiction texts you have read in this unit.
• an explicitly stated claim about the topic.
• a logically organized presentation of sound reasons and textual evidence.
• a conclusion that sums up your literary analysis, evaluates your claims and evidence
  about which text was more persuasive, and leaves your readers with an original
  thought about the topic.

Font   Size   **B** *I* I̲ₓ A A̲ U

The   I'm

NOTES

LITERARY ANALYSIS

WRITING PROMPT

Imagine what it would be like to work long hours under dangerous conditions for little pay. Think about how your life would be different if you had to work in a factory or on a farm as a migrant farm worker, instead of going to school. The world is full of injustice, but fortunately, there are people who believe in speaking up for the powerless and defending human rights.

In this unit, you have been reading nonfiction texts about real people who stood up for the rights of others and brought about social change. From Mother Jones, a fierce fighter for child labor laws, to Cesar Chavez, who fought for the rights of ill-treated farm workers, these great people had something in common: They fought for fairness and inspired social change.

Mahatma Gandhi and Nelson Mandela also fought for change. Both Gandhi and Mandela are inspiring, but the texts that you have read about them are very different. Write a literary analysis in which you compare and contrast the text about Gandhi with the text about Mandela to determine which is more convincing in presenting and supporting the claim that this individual was a great defender of justice and human rights. Analyze the reasons and evidence presented in the text as well as the language that is used to describe the individual's words, actions, and accomplishments. Then decide which writer was more persuasive in defending his claim about the impact this person had on human rights.

Your literary analysis should include

- a comparison-contrast of two nonfiction texts you have read in this unit.

WRITING PROMPT *continued*

- an explicitly stated claim about the topic.
- a logically organized presentation of sound reasons and textual evidence.
- a conclusion that sums up your literary analysis of which text was more persuasive and leaves your readers with an original thought about the topic.

A **literary analysis** considers the themes or central ideas of one or more pieces of literature. It may explain connections between (or among) different texts, between the writer and the text, or between literature and its effect on the reader or a larger audience.

Literary analysis can be a form of argumentative writing: The writer makes a claim about the literature and then provides relevant textual evidence—details, descriptions, examples, observations, and quotations—to support the argument and claims. After first introducing a claim, the writer develops his or her ideas in the body of the literary analysis, using transitions to show connections and create a smooth flow of ideas. Often, the author's purpose for writing a literary analysis is to convince readers that the claims the writer is making are valid.

Therefore, the features of a literary analysis may include the following:

- a comparison-contrast of two literary texts
- an introduction with a thesis statement (or claim), a central idea, and support built on sound reasons and textual evidence
- a text structure that organizes the analysis in a logical way, using clear transitions to create a smooth flow of ideas
- embedded quotations that are cited from the texts or from outside sources
- precise word choice
- a concluding statement that restates the thesis statement (or claim), and that summarizes the central idea (or ideas)

As you work on this Extended Writing Project, you will learn more about crafting each of the elements of a literary analysis.

Please note that excerpts and passages in the StudySync® library and this workbook are intended as touchstones to generate interest in an author's work. The excerpts and passages do not substitute for the reading of entire texts, and StudySync® strongly recommends that students seek out and purchase the whole literary or informational work in order to experience it as the author intended. Links to online resellers are available in our digital library. In addition, complete works may be ordered through an authorized reseller by filling out and returning to StudySync® the order form enclosed in this workbook.

Reading & Writing
Companion

85

MODEL

Before you begin writing your literary analysis, start by reading this essay that one student wrote to a prompt that is slightly different from the one you will use. Instead of writing about Nelson Mandela and Mahatma Gandhi, who will be the subjects of your writing prompt, this student compared and contrasted the unit texts about Mother Jones and Cesar Chavez to see which text was more persuasive. This Student Model will help you identify the features of a literary analysis. As you read, highlight and annotate the features of a literary analysis that the Student Model includes.

Mother Jones and Cesar Chavez: Standing Up for Workers' Rights

You have probably spent your day sitting in a classroom, learning important facts so that you can go to college or get a good job after you graduate from high school. But if you had been born one hundred years ago, you might have ended up working long and hard for meager wages in a factory. Similarly, if you had been born fifty or seventy-five years ago, you might have wound up working in the fields of California instead of getting a good education. Life was unfair for a lot of workers in the early-to-mid-twentieth century, especially for children and migrant farm workers. Two people, however, worked hard to change all that—Mary Harris "Mother" Jones and Cesar Chavez. Both championed the rights of workers and called for laws that guaranteed fair pay, shorter working hours, and better working conditions. Although Jones and Chavez lived very different lives in very different times, both defended workers' rights, Jones defending child workers, Chavez championing the rights of farm laborers. Clearly, the authors of *Mother Jones: Fierce Fighter for Workers' Rights* and *About Cesar* admire their subjects, although this literary analysis will prove the point that Chavez was the greater fighter for human rights. As the authors from the Cesar Chavez Foundation state, "Chavez not only righted many of the injustices that farm workers faced, but he also inspired "Americans from all walks of life."

The author Judith Pinkerton Josephson paints an interesting portrait of Mother Jones as she tells the reader that Jones was seventy-three years old when she decided in June of 1903 to draw attention to the problem of child labor. As Josephson says in paragraph 4, even though it was against the law to hire children younger than 13 to work in factories, "parents often lied about a child's age," and "[m]ill owners "looked the other way, because child labor was cheap." As a result, thousands of children worked long hours under terrible working conditions in mills, with often serious effects to their health. To highlight this point, Josephson notes, in paragraph 3, how Mother Jones noticed that the children's "bodies were bone-thin with hollow chests," and that many of them were maimed, "with their hands [cut] off, some with the thumb missing." The writer explains how Jones led a group of mill children and their parents to Independence Square in Philadelphia, where she called on city officials to think about the real costs of child labor—mangled limbs, lost childhoods, no education. Jones appealed to their sympathies, stating in paragraph 6: "'Philadelphia's mansions were built on the broken bones, the quivering hearts, and the drooping heads of these children.'" But the officials ignored her. Undeterred, she decided that the best way to bring national attention to the plight of child labor was to march 125 miles to President Theodore Roosevelt's summer home in New York. She and many child workers and their families walked the whole way, stopping only to rest and hold rallies. The author admits that in the end, however, Jones did not meet her goal because President Roosevelt refused to see her. As a result, she and the children returned home without having brought about any real changes to child labor laws. In the last paragraph, Josephson sums up: "Though she had not met with the president, Mother Jones had drawn the attention of the nation to the problem of child labor." However, she does not say that national laws to protect child workers came about because of Jones's efforts. In fact, all she says at the end is that the "federal government finally passed a child labor law. . . in 1938—thirty-five years after the march of the mill children." Josephson's portrait of Mother Jones shows a woman who was committed to a cause but not completely successful at promoting change. She includes criticisms, such as that she was self-centered, that people had of Jones. In the end, Josephson fails to persuade her readers that Mother Jones had a huge impact on human rights.

Unlike Josephson, the authors of *About Cesar* are deeply enthusiastic about their subject, Cesar Chavez. In the first paragraph, these authors from the Cesar Chavez Foundation quote Robert F. Kennedy by saying that he called Chavez "'one of the heroic figures of our time.'" They begin their text by introducing Chavez as a "true American hero," a "farm labor leader . . . a community organizer . . . and a crusader for the environment and consumer rights." Later, in paragraph 15, they refer to him as a "unique and humble leader, as well as a great humanitarian and communicator who influenced and inspired millions of Americans from all walks of life." In paragraph 19, they call him "a common man with an uncommon vision." They support their claims with relevant textual evidence of Chavez's achievements. In paragraph 2, they describe how as a boy, he worked in California's "fields, orchards, and vineyards, where he was exposed to the hardships and injustices of farm worker life." Most of the selection explores Chavez's accomplishments as a leader of the migrant labor movement. The authors outline the specifics of Chavez's achievements, on behalf of migrant workers, including the right to form and join unions, such as the United Farm Workers (the UFW), and create contracts that provided rest periods, safe working conditions, clean drinking water, medical care, and pensions. They also point out that he helped to outlaw dangerous pesticides and job discrimination. More importantly, Chavez did all this while bringing people together. The authors explain, in paragraph 15, that the "significance of Cesar's life transcends any one cause or struggle." They say that he helped form "a national and extraordinarily diverse coalition for farm worker boycotts, which included students, middle class consumers, trade unionists, religious activists, and minorities." In fact, they point out that Chavez made people realize that they had a stake in providing migrant workers with a decent way of life. He made people feel special, and his motto "Sí, se puede!" ("Yes, it can be done!") gave people "the faith to believe in themselves."

Both Mother Jones and Cesar Chavez were crusaders in the fight for human rights. They stood up for workers, and their leadership helped millions of people attain a better life. The two texts support the authors' claims that Jones and Chavez were committed people who tried hard to help others. However, *About Cesar* makes a stronger argument. Its authors praise Chavez and describe him as a hard worker, a great leader, and a man who knew how to reach out to others.

Similarly, Josephson admires her subject and shows how Mother Jones was committed to bringing attention to the problem of child labor. But Mother Jones did not have the same successes with workers' rights as did Chavez. In the end, she was not able to persuade lawmakers to improve working conditions for children. In fact, the connection Josephson makes between the 1903 march and the child labor laws enacted in 1938 is not well supported or convincing. She does not provide sufficient evidence to suggest that lawmakers thought about Mother Jones when they passed child labor laws years later. Perhaps because Mother Jones lived so long ago, her human rights efforts seem to have had less impact than those of Chavez, who died in 1993. Although Jones and Chavez both fought to secure workers' rights, Chavez's influence was stronger. Only he improved the lives of workers in his lifetime and "inspired millions of Americans from all walks of life."

 ## THINK QUESTIONS

1. Which sentence in the first paragraph most clearly states what the entire essay will be about?

2. How does the Student Model organize its evidence in the second and third paragraphs? Cite textual evidence to support your response.

3. In the last two paragraphs, what conclusion does the writer reach about which text is more persuasive? How does the writer support this conclusion? Cite specific evidence from the Student Model to support your claim.

4. Think about the writing prompt. Which selections or other resources would you like to use to create your own literary analysis comparing and contrasting the texts that focus on the humanitarian efforts of Mahatma Gandhi and Nelson Mandela? What are some ideas you might want to develop when you compare and contrast your two texts?

5. Based on what you have read, listened to, or researched, how would you answer the question: *Why is it essential to defend human rights?* Support your answer with relevant evidence from the Student Model.

Please note that excerpts and passages in the StudySync® library and this workbook are intended as touchstones to generate interest in an author's work. The excerpts and passages do not substitute for the reading of entire texts, and StudySync® strongly recommends that students seek out and purchase the whole literary or informational work in order to experience it as the author intended. Links to online resellers are available in our digital library. In addition, complete works may be ordered through an authorized reseller by filling out and returning to StudySync® the order form enclosed in this workbook.

Reading & Writing Companion

89

PREWRITE

CA-CCSS: CA.RI.7.1, CA.RI.7.2, CA.RI.7.3, CA.RI.7.9, CA.W.7.1a, CA.W.7.2b, CA.W.7.4, CA.W.7.5, CA.W.7.6, CA.W.7.9b, CA.SL.7.1a, CA.SL.7.1b, CA.SL.7.1c

WRITING PROMPT

Imagine what it would be like to work long hours under dangerous conditions for little pay. Think about how your life would be different if you had to work in a factory or on a farm as a migrant farm worker, instead of going to school. The world is full of injustice, but fortunately, there are people who believe in speaking up for the powerless and defending human rights.

In this unit, you have been reading nonfiction texts about real people who stood up for the rights of others and brought about social change. From Mother Jones, a fierce fighter for child labor laws, to Cesar Chavez, who fought for the rights of ill-treated farm workers, these great people had something in common: They fought for fairness and inspired social change.

Mahatma Gandhi and Nelson Mandela also fought for change. Both Gandhi and Mandela are inspiring, but the texts that you have read about them are very different. Write a literary analysis in which you compare and contrast the text about Gandhi with the text about Mandela to determine which is more convincing in presenting and supporting the claim that this individual was a great defender of justice and human rights. Analyze the reasons and evidence presented in the text as well as the language that is used to describe the individual's words, actions, and accomplishments. Then decide which writer was more persuasive in defending his claim about the impact this person had on human rights.

Your literary analysis should include

- a comparison-contrast of two nonfiction texts you have read in this unit.

WRITING PROMPT *continued*

- an explicitly stated claim about the topic.
- a logically organized presentation of sound reasons and textual evidence.
- a conclusion that sums up your literary analysis of which text was more persuasive and leaves your readers with an original thought about the topic.

You have been reading about humanitarians from different places in history who stood up for the rights of others. In the extended writing project, you will consider two texts about these human rights activists, Mahatma Gandhi and Nelson Mandela. In a literary analysis, you will explore how well the authors presented their claims about their two subjects. You will also trace and evaluate how relevant and sufficient their evidence was in supporting their claims.

Begin by asking yourself these questions: Who were these two people? How did they help others? What made them great? What were the consequences of their actions? How does each author persuade you that his person devoted his life to protecting the human rights of others?

Make a list of the answers to these questions as you read, looking for patterns between the texts. What are the similarities and differences between Gandhi and Mandela? Do the texts treat their subjects in a similar or different way? Do they make similar claims? Is one text more persuasive than the other? How? Identifying patterns, details, claims, and word choice can help you decide what you will want to discuss in your essay. Follow the Student Model to help you get started with the prewriting of your own literary analysis:

Texts: *Mother Jones: Fierce Fighter for Worker's Rights* and *About Cesar*

Similarities and differences between the two subjects: Both Mother Jones and Cesar Chavez stood up for workers who were not paid enough for the hard and dangerous work they performed. Mother Jones led child workers and their parents on a 125-mile march to see President Theodore Roosevelt, but he would not meet with them. Chavez organized a farm workers' union and helped secure laws that made working conditions for migrant farm workers safer and improved the quality of their lives.

Similarities and differences between the texts, the author's claims, and ideas: The writers think that their subjects were great supporters of human rights. The

Please note that excerpts and passages in the StudySync® library and this workbook are intended as touchstones to generate interest in an author's work. The excerpts and passages do not substitute for the reading of entire texts, and StudySync® strongly recommends that students seek out and purchase the whole literary or informational work in order to experience it as the author intended. Links to online resellers are available in our digital library. In addition, complete works may be ordered through an authorized reseller by filling out and returning to StudySync® the order form enclosed in this workbook.

Reading & Writing Companion   **91**

author of the text about Mother Jones recognizes that Jones was not completely successful in helping the child workers. However, the authors of the text about Cesar Chavez are in awe of their subject, praise him, and spell out his many achievements.

Which text is more persuasive, and why: The text about Chavez is more persuasive because it uses sound reasons and relevant, sufficient evidence to support its claim about Chavez's many accomplishments as a fighter for human rights.

SKILL:
THESIS
STATEMENT

DEFINE

In informative writing, a thesis statement expresses a writer's central (or main) idea about a topic. In argumentative writing, a thesis statement takes the form of a claim. The claim is the writer's opinion (or point of view) about the topic. When writing a literary analysis, a writer expresses an opinion about one or more texts. The writer's claim typically appears in the introduction, or first paragraph, of the literary analysis, often as the last sentence. Support for the claim, such as details, examples, observations, and quotations from the text, appears in the body of the essay.

IDENTIFICATION AND APPLICATION

A thesis statement, or claim

- expresses an opinion about one or more texts.
- previews what will appear in the body of the literary analysis.
- addresses all aspects of the writing prompt for the literary analysis.
- appears in the introduction, or the first paragraph.

MODEL

The following is the introduction, or first paragraph, from the Student Model, "Mother Jones and Cesar Chavez: Standing Up for Workers' Rights":

> You have probably spent your day sitting in a classroom, learning important facts, so that you can go to college or get a good job after you graduate from high school. But if you had been born one hundred years ago, you might have ended up working long and hard for meager wages in a factory. Similarly, if you had been born fifty or seventy-five years ago, you might

Please note that excerpts and passages in the StudySync® library and this workbook are intended as touchstones to generate interest in an author's work. The excerpts and passages do not substitute for the reading of entire texts, and StudySync® strongly recommends that students seek out and purchase the whole literary or informational work in order to experience it as the author intended. Links to online resellers are available in our digital library. In addition, complete works may be ordered through an authorized reseller by filling out and returning to StudySync® the order form enclosed in this workbook.

Reading & Writing
Companion

93

have wound up working in the fields of California instead of getting a good education. Life was unfair for a lot of workers in the early-to-mid-twentieth century, especially for children and migrant farm workers. However, two people worked hard to help change all that—Mary Harris "Mother" Jones and Cesar Chavez. Both championed the rights of workers and called for laws that guaranteed fair pay, shorter working hours, and better working conditions. Although Jones and Chavez lived very different lives in very different times, both defended workers' rights, Jones defending child workers, Chavez championing the rights of farm laborers. Clearly, the authors of *Mother Jones: Fierce Fighter for Workers' Rights* and *About Cesar* admire their subjects, although this literary analysis will prove the point that Chavez was the greater fighter for human rights. As the authors from the Cesar Chavez Foundation state, "Chavez not only righted many of the injustices that farm workers faced, but he also inspired "Americans from all walks of life."

As you reread this excerpt from the first paragraph of the Student Model, look for the thesis statement, or student's claim. The student's claim responds to the writing prompt by identifying the texts he or she has examined. It also states his or her opinion (or point of view) about which text is more persuasive and why.

 PRACTICE

Write a thesis statement for your literary analysis that states your claim as it relates to the writing prompt. When you have finished, share your thesis statement with a partner and offer each other constructive feedback.

SKILL:
ORGANIZE
ARGUMENTATIVE
WRITING

DEFINE

A literary analysis can be a form of argumentative writing that tries to persuade readers to accept the writer's opinion of a particular text (or texts). To write such a literary analysis, the writer must organize and present the reasons and relevant evidence—the facts, details, examples, and quotations from the text (or texts)—in a logical and convincing way. In addition, the writer must choose an organizational (or text) structure that best suits the argument.

The writer of a literary analysis can choose from a number of organizational structures in which to couch the argument, including compare and contrast, order of importance, problem and solution, cause and effect, and sequential (chronological, or time) order. Experienced writers use an outline or another graphic organizer to decide how to order and convey their ideas persuasively.

IDENTIFICATION AND APPLICATION

- When selecting an overall organizational structure for a literary analysis, a writer must consider his or her argument or specific claims about the text (or texts). Then the writer must think about the best way of presenting the supporting evidence. He or she can do this by asking these questions:
  - › To support my idea, will I compare and contrast ideas or details in the text?
  - › Is there an order of importance to my evidence? Does all my evidence support my claim equally well? Is some evidence stronger?
  - › Will I raise a question or identify a problem in my argument? Do I have supporting evidence that suggests a solution or an answer?
  - › Does my supporting evidence suggest a cause-and-effect relationship?
  - › To support my claim, does it make sense to retell the events in sequential (or chronological) order?

Please note that excerpts and passages in the StudySync® library and this workbook are intended as touchstones to generate interest in an author's work. The excerpts and passages do not substitute for the reading of entire texts, and StudySync® strongly recommends that students seek out and purchase the whole literary or informational work in order to experience it as the author intended. Links to online resellers are available in our digital library. In addition, complete works may be ordered through an authorized reseller by filling out and returning to StudySync® the order form enclosed in this workbook.

Reading & Writing
Companion

95

- Writers often use specific signal (or transition) words or phrases to help readers recognize the organizational structure or pattern of their writing. Here are some examples of transitions:
  › Compare and contrast: *like, similarly, in the same way* to compare and *unlike, different from, although, while, but, however, on the other hand* to contrast
  › Order of importance: *most, most important, least, least important, mainly*
  › Problem and solution: *problem, solution, why, how*
  › Cause and effect: *because, therefore, as a result, cause, effect, so*
  › Chronological order: *first, next, then, finally, last, during that time,*

- Writers are not limited to using only one organizational pattern throughout a text. Within a specific section or paragraph, they might use a different text structure. This does not affect the overall organization, however.

MODEL

During the prewriting stage, the writer of the Student Model understood that the assignment required him or her to compare and contrast two texts from the unit in order to determine which text was more persuasive. The writer knew that that would involve weighing the claims and evidence from both texts in order to decide which author was more persuasive in showing that the subject of the text was the greater defender of human rights. Therefore, an overall compare-and-contrast organizational structure best suited this writer's argument.

In this excerpt from the Student Model, the author uses a compare/contrast text structure:

> **Unlike Josephson,** the authors of *About Cesar* are deeply enthusiastic about their subject, Cesar Chavez. In the first paragraph, these authors from the Cesar Chavez Foundation quote Robert F. Kennedy by saying that he called Chavez "'one of the heroic figures of our time.'"

Once a writer has selected the most appropriate organizational structure, he or she can use an outline or a graphic organizer (for example, a Venn diagram, concept map, or flowchart) to begin organizing the supporting evidence that will back up his or her claim.

The writer of the Student Model used this graphic organizer during planning to organize the evidence to support this claim: The authors of *About Chavez* were more persuasive than the author of *Mother Jones: Fierce Fighter for Workers' Rights* in showing that their subject was the greater fighter for human rights.

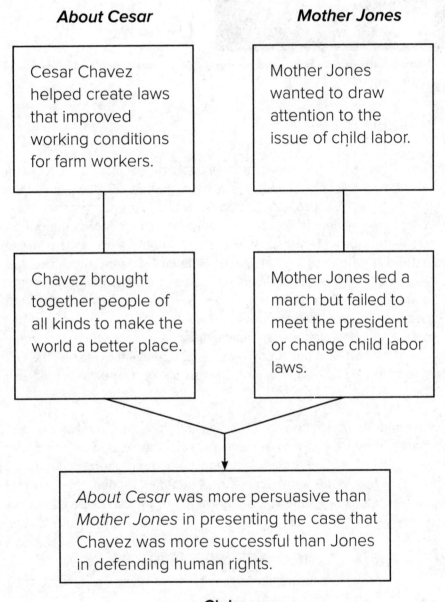

About Cesar

Cesar Chavez helped create laws that improved working conditions for farm workers.

Chavez brought together people of all kinds to make the world a better place.

Mother Jones

Mother Jones wanted to draw attention to the issue of child labor.

Mother Jones led a march but failed to meet the president or change child labor laws.

About Cesar was more persuasive than *Mother Jones* in presenting the case that Chavez was more successful than Jones in defending human rights.

Claim

 PRACTICE

By using an *Organize Argumentative Writing* graphic organizer like the one used with the Student Model, you'll be able to fill in the information you gathered in the Prewrite stage. Now that you've organized or structured your literary analysis, you'll soon be able to begin your own literary analysis.

SKILL:
SUPPORTING
DETAILS

 DEFINE

Because a literary analysis makes a claim about one or more texts, it is a form of argumentative writing. To make his or her argument effective, the writer of a literary analysis must provide supporting details in the form of reasons and relevant textual evidence. Reasons are statements that answer the question "Why?" Writers provide reasons to support a claim and to help readers understand their analysis of the texts. Relevant evidence includes facts, definitions, quotations, observations, and examples from the text (or texts) being analyzed or from outside sources. Relevant evidence is key to the success of the writer's argument. It makes the literary analysis more persuasive, develops the ideas, and clarifies the writer's understanding and analysis of the text. Without strong reasons and relevant evidence, the writer would simply be stating his or her opinion about the texts without using support.

Because writers want to convince readers that their interpretation of a text is believable, they carefully select and present the evidence. Evidence is relevant only if it supports the claim and helps build the argument. If the evidence—a fact, detail, an example, or a quotation—does not support the claim or validate the argument, it is irrelevant and should not be used.

 IDENTIFICATION AND APPLICATION

Step 1:

Review your claim. To identify supporting details that are relevant to your claim, ask the following questions:

- What am I trying to persuade my audience (or readers) to believe?
- What kinds of supporting details—reasons and evidence—can I include that will help persuade them?

Step 2:

Ask what your reader needs to know about the topic in order to understand your claim. Think about the reasons you'll need to provide as evidence to convince your readers that your claim is valid.

Step 3:

Look for facts, definitions, quotations, observations, examples, and descriptions from the texts you are analyzing or from outside sources you are using as evidence. Use supporting details such as these to build on ideas you've already provided, but remember to evaluate their relevance to your argument and claims. To do this, ask yourself these questions:

- Does this detail help my reader understand the topic?
- Does this detail support my claim?
- Can I use it as evidence to help build, support, or reinforce my argument?
- Is there stronger evidence that makes the same point?

 MODEL

In the following excerpt from the first paragraph from *About Cesar,* the authors provide supporting details to back up their claim that Chavez was a "true American hero . . . a civil rights, Latino and farm labor leader . . . a community organizer and social entrepreneur; a champion of militant nonviolent social change; and a crusader for the environment and consumer rights."

In paragraph 15, the authors provide evidence that Chavez was an effective labor leader. They offer specific details about the union he helped organize and how it influenced migrant farm workers and others.

> The significance of Cesar's life transcends any one cause or struggle. He was a unique and humble leader, as well as a great humanitarian and communicator who influenced and inspired millions of Americans from all walks of life. **Cesar forged a national and extraordinarily diverse coalition for farm worker boycotts, which included students, middle class consumers, trade unionists, religious activists and minorities.**

Here, the authors support the claim that Chavez was a strong labor leader and community organizer. They tell how he brought together people from different professions and classes to support the cause of the farm workers. The authors list the specific kinds of people who were involved in Chavez's cause. Then, in paragraph 18, the authors employ further evidence:

> Cesar liked to say that his job as an organizer was helping ordinary people do extraordinary things. **Cesar made everyone, especially the**

Please note that excerpts and passages in the StudySync® library and this workbook are intended as touchstones to generate interest in an author's work. The excerpts and passages do not substitute for the reading of entire texts, and StudySync® strongly recommends that students seek out and purchase the whole literary or informational work in order to experience it as the author intended. Links to online resellers are available in our digital library. In addition, complete works may be ordered through an authorized reseller by filling out and returning to StudySync® the order form enclosed in this workbook.

Reading & Writing Companion

99

farm workers, feel the jobs they were doing in the movement were very important. It did not matter if they were lawyers working in the courtrooms or cooks in the kitchen feeding the people involved in the strike, he showed the farm workers that they could win against great odds. He gave people the faith to believe in themselves, even if they were poor and unable to receive the best education.

Here, the authors give specific examples of how Chavez led people by bringing them together—by making them feel that despite the role they played in the movement, everyone was important and essential in the fight to secure human rights.

EXTENDED WRITING PROJECT
PLAN

PLAN

CA-CCSS: CA.RI.7.1, CA.RI.7.8, CA.W.7.1a, CA.W.7.1b, CA.W.7.5, CA.W.7.6, CA.SL.7.1a, CA.SL.7.1c, CA.SL.7.2

WRITING PROMPT

Imagine what it would be like to work long hours under dangerous conditions for little pay. Think about how your life would be different if you had to work in a factory or on a farm as a migrant farm worker, instead of going to school. The world is full of injustice, but fortunately, there are people who believe in speaking up for the powerless and defending human rights.

In this unit, you have been reading nonfiction texts about real people who stood up for the rights of others and brought about social change. From Mother Jones, a fierce fighter for child labor laws, to Cesar Chavez, who fought for the rights of ill-treated farm workers, these great people had something in common: They fought for fairness and inspired social change.

Mahatma Gandhi and Nelson Mandela also fought for change. Both Gandhi and Mandela are inspiring, but the texts that you have read about them are very different. Write a literary analysis in which you compare and contrast the text about Gandhi with the text about Mandela to determine which is more convincing in presenting and supporting the claim that this individual was a great defender of justice and human rights. Analyze the reasons and evidence presented in the text as well as the language that is used to describe the individual's words, actions, and accomplishments. Then decide which writer was more persuasive in defending his claim about the impact this person had on human rights.

Your literary analysis should include

- a comparison-contrast of two nonfiction texts you have read in this unit.

Please note that excerpts and passages in the StudySync® library and this workbook are intended as touchstones to generate interest in an author's work. The excerpts and passages do not substitute for the reading of entire texts, and StudySync® strongly recommends that students seek out and purchase the whole literary or informational work in order to experience it as the author intended. Links to online resellers are available in our digital library. In addition, complete works may be ordered through an authorized reseller by filling out and returning to StudySync® the order form enclosed in this workbook.

Reading & Writing Companion   101

WRITING PROMPT *continued*

- an explicitly stated claim about the topic.
- a logically organized presentation of sound reasons and textual evidence.
- a conclusion that sums up your literary analysis of which text was more persuasive and leaves your readers with an original thought about the topic.

Review the information you listed in your *Organize Argumentative Writing* graphic organizer in which you cited evidence from *About Chavez* and *Mother Jones: Fierce Fighter for Workers' Rights*. This completed organizer, with its filled-in details from the two texts, along with your claim, will help you create a road map to use for writing your literary analysis.

Consider the following questions as you develop your body paragraphs and their supporting details in your road map:

- Who are the subjects of the texts? What did they accomplish?
- To what degree do the authors think their subjects are supporters of human rights? How do you know?
- What attitude does each author have toward human rights?
- How persuasive is each author in presenting his or her ideas?
- Which text did you ultimately find more persuasive?
- Why were you persuaded in favor of one person over the other?

Use this model to get started with your road map:

Literary Analysis Road Map

Claim: *About Cesar* is more persuasive than *Mother Jones: Fierce Fighter for Workers' Rights* in presenting the case that its subject was a great supporter of human rights.

Body Paragraph 1 Topic: Mother Jones wanted to draw attention to the issue of child labor.

> **Supporting Detail #1:** She led the mill children and their parents on a 125-mile march to meet President Theodore Roosevelt.

Supporting Detail #2: The president would not see Jones and the children, and they returned home without bringing about any change to child labor laws.

Body Paragraph 2 Topic: Cesar Chavez dedicated his life to helping migrant farm workers gain rights and improve their lives.

Supporting Detail #1: Under Chavez's leadership, the United Farm Workers (UFW), a labor union for farm workers in the United States, became the first successful union for farm workers in American history, offering benefits to workers.

Supporting Detail #2: Chavez brought people from all walks of life together to support the cause of the migrant farm workers.

Body Paragraph 3 Topic: The text about Cesar Chavez was more persuasive than the text about Mother Jones.

Supporting Detail #1: Mother Jones felt strongly about enacting child labor laws and improving the lives of child workers, but the author was unable to show how effective Jones's efforts were in bringing about any real change during her lifetime.

Supporting Detail #2: The authors were able to show that Cesar Chavez greatly improved the lives of farm workers, enabling them to join unions and gain workers' rights, and they provided evidence to show that many people considered Chavez to be "a great leader."

Please note that excerpts and passages in the StudySync® library and this workbook are intended as touchstones to generate interest in an author's work. The excerpts and passages do not substitute for the reading of entire texts, and StudySync® strongly recommends that students seek out and purchase the whole literary or informational work in order to experience it as the author intended. Links to online resellers are available in our digital library. In addition, complete works may be ordered through an authorized reseller by filling out and returning to StudySync® the order form enclosed in this workbook.

Reading & Writing Companion   **103**

NOTES

INTRODUCTIONS
sync-skills

SKILL:
INTRODUCTIONS

 DEFINE

The **introduction** is the opening paragraph or section of a literary analysis. It identifies the texts and the topic to be discussed, states the writer's claim, and previews the supporting evidence that will appear in the body of the text. The introduction is also the place where most writers include a "hook" that is intended to "grab" the reader's attention and connect the reader to the text.

 IDENTIFICATION AND APPLICATION

- In a literary analysis, the introduction is usually the first paragraph or section, and it is where the writer identifies the text (or texts) or topic to be analyzed. Since a literary analysis examines one or more texts in depth, the writer must let readers know what the focus of the analysis will be.

- A literary analysis is a form of argument, so the writer's specific claim is an important part of the introduction. The claim is a direct statement of the writer's opinion of the texts under discussion. By stating the claim in the introduction, the writer lets the reader know the ideas or opinion he or she will explore. Establishing a claim in the introduction also allows readers to form their own opinions, which they can then measure against the writer's opinion as they read.

- Another use of the introduction is to provide a preview of the textual evidence which readers will later assess to determine whether it is relevant and sufficient to support the writer's claim.

- The introduction enables the writer to establish an effective argument, increasing the likelihood that readers will agree with his or her claim.

- A good introduction contains a "hook" that leaves readers with a first impression about what to expect from the writer. Good hooks engage readers' interest and make them want to keep reading.

MODEL

NOTES

The introductory section of Barbara Jordan's keynote address to the 1976 Democratic National Convention, which appears in this unit, contains the key elements of a good introduction. Read Jordan's introduction closely to see how she "hooks" her readers and establishes her claim.

Thank you ladies and gentlemen for a very warm reception.

It was one hundred and forty-four years ago that members of the Democratic Party first met in convention to select a Presidential candidate. Since that time, Democrats have continued to convene once every four years and draft a party platform and nominate a Presidential candidate. And our meeting this week is a continuation of that tradition. But there is something different about tonight. **There is something special about tonight. What is different? What is special?**

I, Barbara Jordan, am a keynote speaker.

A lot of years passed since 1832, and during that time it would have been most unusual for any national political party to ask a Barbara Jordan to deliver a keynote address. But tonight, here I am. And I feel that notwithstanding the past that my presence here is one additional bit of evidence that the American Dream need not forever be deferred.

Now that I have this grand distinction, what in the world am I supposed to say? . . . I could list the many problems which Americans have. I could list the problems which cause people to feel cynical, angry, frustrated: problems which include lack of integrity in government; the feeling that the individual no longer counts; the reality of material and spiritual poverty; the feeling that the grand American experiment is failing or has failed. I could recite these problems, and then I could sit down and offer no solutions. But I don't choose to do that either. The citizens of America expect more. They deserve and they want more than a recital of problems.

We are a people in a quandary about the present. We are a people in search of our future. We are a people in search of a national community. We are a people trying not only to solve the problems of the present, unemployment, inflation, but we are attempting on a larger scale to fulfill the promise of America. **We are attempting to fulfill our national purpose, to create and sustain a society in which all of us are equal.**

In her introduction, Jordan uses an effective **hook**. She engages her audience by making an observation, repeating words and phrases for emphasis, and then posing questions: "But there is something different about tonight. There is something special about tonight. What is different? What is special?" Then she makes her proclamation: " I, Barbara Jordan, am a keynote speaker." She continues: "Now that I have this grand distinction, what in the world am I supposed to say?" Jordan's answers to these questions lead to her **claim**— that her presence as the keynote speaker indicates that for African American women, the American Dream is no longer "deferred"—that the United States is beginning to "fulfill our national purpose, to create and sustain a society in which all of us are equal." Jordan's introduction also hints at the **relevant evidence** that will follow in the body of her speech. This evidence is likely to contain historical facts about the American political process, referring to the current woes of the day, such as cynicism, unemployment, and inflation, along with suggestions for ways to solve the nation's problems.

 ## PRACTICE

Write an introduction for your literary analysis that includes your claim and a "hook" to capture your readers' interest. When you have finished, trade your paper with a partner. Participate in a peer review of each other's introduction and hook, and offer thoughtful, constructive, and supportive feedback to your partner.

SKILL: BODY
PARAGRAPHS
AND
TRANSITIONS

 DEFINE

Body paragraphs appear between the introduction and the conclusion—between the beginning and the end—of an essay. They are also called middle paragraphs, because they appear in the middle of a text, and this middle section is the "meaty" part of any literary analysis. It is where you support your specific claims with sound reasons and relevant evidence that in turn will be sufficient enough to support your argument. In general, each body paragraph should focus on one main point, central idea, or claim so that your readers can easily follow your thinking. All the main points of the body paragraphs should collectively support the argument of your literary analysis.

It is important to structure each body paragraph clearly. One way to structure a body paragraph of a literary analysis is by including the following elements:

Topic sentence: The topic sentence is the first sentence of a body paragraph. It states the paragraph's central idea and should relate to the main point of your claim.

Evidence #1: Each middle paragraph will contain evidence from the text (or texts) you are analyzing to support the topic sentence of the body paragraph. Textual evidence can include relevant definitions, details, facts, observations, quotations, and examples.

Evidence #2: Continue to develop your claim or central idea of the body paragraph with a second piece of evidence. This evidence may come from outside research you have done on the topic or from the source texts you are comparing and contrasting.

Analysis/Explanation: After presenting your evidence, explain how it helps to support your topic sentence—and main claim—about the texts you are analyzing.

Please note that excerpts and passages in the StudySync® library and this workbook are intended as touchstones to generate interest in an author's work. The excerpts and passages do not substitute for the reading of entire texts, and StudySync® strongly recommends that students seek out and purchase the whole literary or informational work in order to experience it as the author intended. Links to online resellers are available in our digital library. In addition, complete works may be ordered through an authorized reseller by filling out and returning to StudySync® the order form enclosed in this workbook.

Reading & Writing
Companion   **107**

Concluding sentence: After presenting your evidence, restate your main claim and summarize the central idea you have made in the topic sentence of each body paragraph.

Transitions are connecting words or phrases that writers use to clarify the relationships between (or among) ideas in a text. Transitions help connect words in a sentence and ideas in individual paragraphs. They also suggest the organizational structure of a text.

Connecting words such as *and, or,* and *but* help writers make connections between (or among) words in a sentence, while words and phrases such as also, *in addition,* and *likewise* show how ideas in body paragraphs relate. Adding transition words or phrases to the beginning or end of a paragraph can help a writer guide readers smoothly through a text. Transitions can also indicate the organizational structure being used by the writer to present the evidence or ideas.

 ## IDENTIFICATION AND APPLICATION

- Body paragraphs are the section of the literary analysis between the introduction and the conclusion. These paragraphs provide the main points of the literary analysis, along with the supporting evidence. Typically, writers develop one central idea or claim for each body paragraph.
  - › A topic sentence clearly states the central idea or claim of that paragraph.
  - › Evidence consists of relevant definitions, details, facts, observations, quotations, and examples.
  - › Analysis and explanation tell how the evidence supports the topic sentence.
  - › A concluding sentence summarizes the paragraph's central idea or claim.

- Certain transition words and phrases indicate the organizational structure of a text. Here are some examples of transitions used to organize text in a specific way:
  - › Cause-effect: *because, since, therefore, as a result, so, if . . . then*
  - › Compare and contrast: *likewise, also, both, similarly, in the same way* to compare, and *although, while, but, however, whereas, on the contrary* to contrast
  - › Chronological order: *first, next, then, finally, before, after, within a few years*

- Transitions also help readers understand the relationships between (or among) ideas in a text. A phrase such as *for example* can help show the relationship between a central idea or claim and its evidence. The phrase *in addition* can help link together similar ideas.

 MODEL

Read the first body paragraph from the Student Model, "Mother Jones and Cesar Chavez: Standing Up for Workers' Rights." Look closely at the organizational structure and note the transition words and phrases in bold. Think about the effectiveness of the paragraph. Does it develop the main point of the claim made in the topic sentence? How do the transition words and phrases help you understand how the text is structured and how the ideas are related?

> The author Judith Pinkerton Josephson paints an interesting portrait of Mother Jones as she tells the reader that Jones was seventy-three years old when she decided in June of 1903 to draw attention to the problem of child labor. As Josephson says in paragraph 4, **even though** it was against the law to hire children younger than 13 to work in factories, "parents often lied about a child's age," and "[m]ill owners "looked the other way, **because** child labor was cheap." **As a result,** thousands of children worked long hours under terrible working conditions in mills, with often serious effects to their health. To highlight this point, Josephson notes in paragraph 3 how Mother Jones noticed that the children's "bodies were bone-thin with hollow chests," and that many children were maimed, "with their hands [cut] off, some with the thumb missing." The writer explains how Jones led a group of mill children and their parents to Independence Square in Philadelphia, where she called on city officials to think about the real costs of child labor—mangled limbs, lost childhoods, no education. Jones appealed to their sympathies, stating in paragraph 6: "'Philadelphia's mansions were built on the broken bones, the quivering hearts, and the drooping heads of these children.'" **But** the officials ignored her. Undeterred, she decided that the best way to bring national attention to the plight of child labor was to march 125 miles to President Theodore Roosevelt's summer home in New York. She and many child workers and their families walked the whole way, stopping only to rest and hold rallies. The author admits that **in the end, however,** Jones did not meet her goal **because** President Roosevelt refused to see her. **As a result,** she and

the children returned home without having brought about any real changes to child labor laws. In the last paragraph, Josephson sums up: "**Though** she had not met with the president, Mother Jones had drawn the attention of the nation to the problem of child labor. " **However**, she does not say that national laws to protect child workers came about **because** of Jones's efforts. In fact, all she says at the end is that is that "[t]he federal government finally passed a child labor law . . . in 1938--thirty-five years after the march of the mill children." Josephson's portrait of Mother Jones shows a woman who was committed to a cause but not completely successful at promoting change. . . . **In the end,** Josephson fails to persuade her readers that Mother Jones had a huge impact on human rights.

Remember that the final sentences of the introduction of the Student Model make this claim:

Clearly, the authors of *Mother Jones: Fierce Fighter for Workers' Rights* and *About Cesar* admire their subjects, although this literary analysis will prove the point that Chavez was the greater fighter for human rights. As the authors from the Cesar Chavez Foundation state, "Chavez not only righted many of the injustices that farm workers faced, but he also inspired "Americans from all walks of life."

How does the body paragraph about Mother Jones connect to this claim? Let's take a look.

The **topic sentence** establishes that the first body paragraph will examine the text about Mother Jones. The writer follows the topic sentence with evidence in the paragraph that provides background information about Mother Jones and the issue of child labor. The writer tells about Mother Jones's role in the rally in Philadelphia's Independence Square and the march to President Roosevelt's summer home, and provides facts and quotations from the source text.

Next, the writer **explains** the significance of Mother Jones's efforts. She tells how Jones was unable to meet with President Roosevelt but still put a spotlight on the horrors of child labor. The paragraph concludes by saying that in the end, Josephson "fails to persuade her readers that Mother Jones had a huge impact on human rights." This **concluding sentence** wraps up the body paragraph. It also ties back to the claim—that the text about Chavez was more effective than the text about Mother Jones in making a case that its subject was the greater humanitarian.

Copyright © BookheadEd Learning, LLC

The writer uses **transition words and phrases** such as "but," "however," "even though," "because," "as a result," and "in the end" within the paragraph to show connections (contrasts, causes and effects, and chronological order) as well as the organization of the text. The transition words also guide readers from one sentence and idea to the next by creating a smooth flow of ideas.

PRACTICE

Write one body paragraph for your literary analysis that follows the suggested format. When you are finished, trade with a partner and offer each other feedback. How effective is the topic sentence at stating the main point of the paragraph? How strong is the evidence used to support the topic sentence? Are all quotes and evidence cited correctly? Does the literary analysis support the topic sentence and the claim? Offer each other suggestions, and remember that feedback is most helpful when it is constructive and supportive.

Please note that excerpts and passages in the StudySync® library and this workbook are intended as touchstones to generate interest in an author's work. The excerpts and passages do not substitute for the reading of entire texts, and StudySync® strongly recommends that students seek out and purchase the whole literary or informational work in order to experience it as the author intended. Links to online resellers are available in our digital library. In addition, complete works may be ordered through an authorized reseller by filling out and returning to StudySync® the order form enclosed in this workbook.

Reading & Writing Companion

111

SKILL : CONCLUSIONS

 DEFINE

The **conclusion** is the closing statement or section of a nonfiction text. In a literary analysis, the conclusion brings the writer's argument to a close. It follows directly from the introduction and the body paragraphs by referring to the ideas presented there. The conclusion should restate the thesis statement (or claim) made in the introduction and summarize the central ideas covered in the body paragraphs. In addition, the conclusion should focus on the writer's most convincing reasons and strongest evidence. A conclusion that emphasizes the strongest points of a literary analysis will be more likely to get readers to agree with the writer's claim. To put it simply, in a literary analysis, the conclusion wraps up the writer's argument, but it may leave the reader with an intriguing question, insight, or inspiring message.

 IDENTIFICATION AND APPLICATION

- An effective conclusion of a literary analysis will restate the writer's claim about one or more texts.

- The conclusion should briefly summarize the strongest and most convincing reasons and evidence from the body paragraphs. Focusing on the strongest points makes it more likely that readers will agree with the writer's claim.

- Some conclusions offer a recommendation or some form of insight relating to the analysis. This may take any of the following forms:

  › An answer to a question first posed in the introduction
  › A question designed to elicit reflection on the part of the reader
  › A memorable or inspiring message
  › A last compelling example
  › A suggestion that readers learn more.

MODEL

In the concluding paragraph of the Student Model, "Mother Jones and Cesar Chavez: Standing Up for Workers' Rights," the writer reinforces the main claim, reminds readers of the central ideas of the literary analysis, and ends with an insightful observation. Reread the student's conclusion:

> Similarly, Josephson admires her subject and shows how Mother Jones was committed to bringing attention to the problem of child labor. But Mother Jones did not have the same successes with workers' rights as did Chavez. In the end, she was not able to persuade lawmakers to improve working conditions for children. In fact, the connection Josephson makes between the 1903 march and the child labor laws enacted in 1938 is not well supported or convincing. She does not provide sufficient evidence to suggest that lawmakers thought about Mother Jones when they passed child labor laws years later. Perhaps because Mother Jones lived so long ago, her human rights efforts seem to have had less impact than those of Chavez, who died in 1993. Although Jones and Chavez both fought to secure workers' rights, Chavez's influence was stronger. Only he improved the lives of workers in his lifetime and "inspired millions of Americans from all walks of life."

Remember that the claim in the introduction of the Student Model states the writer's argument: Clearly, the authors of *Mother Jones: Fierce Fighter for Workers' Rights* and *About Cesar* admire their subjects, although this literary analysis will prove the point that Chavez was the greater fighter for human rights. As the authors from the Cesar Chavez Foundation state, "Chavez not only righted many of the injustices that farm workers faced, but he also inspired "Americans from all walks of life."

The text about Cesar Chavez makes a stronger case than the text about Mother Jones for its subject's importance as a humanitarian. The conclusion restates that claim, as well as the reasons and evidence that support it. At the end of the paragraph, the writer leaves the reader with an original thought—that perhaps Mother Jones's human rights' efforts seem less inspiring than Chavez's because she lived a long time ago. It might suggest that the writer has a bias toward events that have occurred more recently, which is something that readers should consider when reflecting on the writer's overall argument.

Please note that excerpts and passages in the StudySync® library and this workbook are intended as touchstones to generate interest in an author's work. The excerpts and passages do not substitute for the reading of entire texts, and StudySync® strongly recommends that students seek out and purchase the whole literary or informational work in order to experience it as the author intended. Links to online resellers are available in our digital library. In addition, complete works may be ordered through an authorized reseller by filling out and returning to StudySync® the order form enclosed in this workbook.

Reading & Writing Companion   113

NOTES

PRACTICE

Write a conclusion for your literary analysis. Your conclusion should include a restatement of the claim on which you have already worked as well as a final thought you might wish to impart to your readers. When you have finished writing your conclusion, trade your work with a partner. Participate in a peer review of your conclusion and offer constructive feedback.

DRAFT

CA-CCSS: CA.RI.7.1, CA.RI.7.8, CA.W.7.1a, CA.W.7.1b, CA.W.7.1c, CA.W.7.1e, CA.W.7.4, CA.W.7.5, CA.W.7.6, CA.W.7.9b, CA.SL.7.1a, CA.SL.7.1b, CA.SL.7.1c, CA.SL.7.1d

WRITING PROMPT

Imagine what it would be like to work long hours under dangerous conditions for little pay. Think about how your life would be different if you had to work in a factory or on a farm as a migrant farm worker, instead of going to school. The world is full of injustice, but fortunately, there are people who believe in speaking up for the powerless and defending human rights.

In this unit, you have been reading nonfiction texts about real people who stood up for the rights of others and brought about social change. From Mother Jones, a fierce fighter for child labor laws, to Cesar Chavez, who fought for the rights of ill-treated farm workers, these great people had something in common: They fought for fairness and inspired social change.

Mahatma Gandhi and Nelson Mandela also fought for change. Both Gandhi and Mandela are inspiring, but the texts that you have read about them are very different. Write a literary analysis in which you compare and contrast the text about Gandhi with the text about Mandela to determine which is more convincing in presenting and supporting the claim that this individual was a great defender of justice and human rights. Analyze the reasons and evidence presented in the text as well as the language that is used to describe the individual's words, actions, and accomplishments. Then decide which writer was more persuasive in defending his claim about the impact this person had on human rights.

Your literary analysis should include

- a comparison-contrast of two nonfiction texts you have read in this unit.

NOTES

> ## WRITING PROMPT *continued*
>
> - an explicitly stated claim about the topic.
> - a logically organized presentation of sound reasons and textual evidence.
> - a conclusion that sums up your literary analysis of which text was more persuasive and leaves your readers with an original thought about the topic.

You have already begun working on your literary analysis. You have considered your purpose, audience, and topic. You have carefully examined the two unit texts you will write about. Based on your analysis of textual evidence, you have identified what you want to say how you will say it. You have decided how to organize your information, and you've gathered supporting details in the form of reasons and relevant evidence. Now it's time to write a draft of your literary analysis.

Use your road map and your other prewriting materials to help you as you write. Remember that a literary analysis begins with an introduction that states a claim (or opinion) and draws readers into the topic. Body paragraphs then develop the claim by providing supporting, relevant evidence, such as facts, details, quotations, examples, and observations. Transitions reinforce the organizational structure and help readers understand the relationships between (or among) ideas. A concluding paragraph restates your main claim and summarizes your main points, or central idea. An insight or intriguing question may be included at the end, making an interesting "takeaway" for your readers.

When drafting your literary analysis, ask yourself these questions:

- How can I "hook" my readers in the introduction?
- How well do I state my claim? Is it clear? Does it state my opinion about the two texts?
- Which textual evidence—including relevant facts, details, quotations, examples, and observations—best supports my claim? Is my evidence sufficient? Are my reasons persuasive?
- How can I improve my organization and flow of ideas by using transitions?
- How can I use a stronger topic sentence in each of my body paragraphs?

- How can I restate my thesis statement (or claim) in the conclusion so that it is clearer and more effective?
- What final insight do I want to leave with my readers?

Be sure to read your draft carefully before you submit it. You'll want to make sure you've addressed every part of the writing prompt so that your literary analysis will be as persuasive as possible.

NOTES

REVISE

CA-CCSS: CA.RI.7.1, CA.W.7.1a, CA.W.7.1b, CA.W.7.1c, CA.W.7.1d, CA.W.7.1e, CA.W.7.4, CA.W.7.5, CA.W.7.6, CA.W.7.9b, CA.W.7.10, CA.SL.7.1a, CA.SL.7.1b, CA.SL.7.1c, CA.SL.7.1d, CA.L.7.1b, CA.L.7.3a

WRITING PROMPT

Imagine what it would be like to work long hours under dangerous conditions for little pay. Think about how your life would be different if you had to work in a factory or on a farm as a migrant farm worker, instead of going to school. The world is full of injustice, but fortunately, there are people who believe in speaking up for the powerless and defending human rights.

In this unit, you have been reading nonfiction texts about real people who stood up for the rights of others and brought about social change. From Mother Jones, a fierce fighter for child labor laws, to Cesar Chavez, who fought for the rights of ill-treated farm workers, these great people had something in common: They fought for fairness and inspired social change.

Mahatma Gandhi and Nelson Mandela also fought for change. Both Gandhi and Mandela are inspiring, but the texts that you have read about them are very different. Write a literary analysis in which you compare and contrast the text about Gandhi with the text about Mandela to determine which is more convincing in presenting and supporting the claim that this individual was a great defender of justice and human rights. Analyze the reasons and evidence presented in the text as well as the language that is used to describe the individual's words, actions, and accomplishments. Then decide which writer was more persuasive in defending his claim about the impact this person had on human rights.

Your literary analysis should include

- a comparison-contrast of two nonfiction texts you have read in this unit.

Copyright © BookheadEd Learning, LLC

WRITING PROMPT *continued*

- an explicitly stated claim about the topic.
- a logically organized presentation of sound reasons and textual evidence.
- a conclusion that sums up your literary analysis of which text was more persuasive and leaves your readers with an original thought about the topic.

You have written a draft of your literary analysis. You have also received input from your peers about how to improve it. Now you are going to revise your draft.

Here are some recommendations to help you revise the draft of your literary analysis:

- Review the suggestions made by your peers.
- Focus on maintaining a formal style. A formal style suits your purpose and audience. Your purpose for writing is to persuade your readers to agree with your opinions about two unit texts. A formal style is also appropriate for your audience: Your audience may be your teacher, your classmates, your family or friends, or other readers who might want to know more about your topic.
- As you revise your draft, eliminate any informal language, such as slang or colloquial expressions, and pay close attention to your use of voice, sentence structure and sentence variety, correct punctuation, and word choice.
  › Remove any first-person pronouns such as *I, me,* or *mine* or instances of addressing readers as *you*, except when leaving readers with a final thought or message in the conclusion.
  › Incorporate varying sentence structure and sentence variety, including long and short sentences, and check that you aren't beginning every sentence in the same way. Also, check that you have punctuated all simple, compound, complex, and compound-complex sentences correctly.
- Does your writing express your ideas precisely and concisely? When it comes to formal writing, less is often more. Look for wordiness and repetition in your writing. Are the exact same ideas repeated more than once? Can you substitute a more exact word for a word that is too

Please note that excerpts and passages in the StudySync® library and this workbook are intended as touchstones to generate interest in an author's work. The excerpts and passages do not substitute for the reading of entire texts, and StudySync® strongly recommends that students seek out and purchase the whole literary or informational work in order to experience it as the author intended. Links to online resellers are available in our digital library. In addition, complete works may be ordered through an authorized reseller by filling out and returning to StudySync® the order form enclosed in this workbook.

Reading & Writing Companion

119

general or overused? Can you replace a longer phrase with a word that means the same thing?

- After you have revised your elements of style, review your literary analysis to see whether you can make improvements to its content or organization.

  › Do you need to add any relevant textual evidence, such as quotations or examples, to fully support your claim?

  › Do you need to incorporate any academic vocabulary or persuasive language that would be appropriate for a literary analysis?

  › Is your organizational structure apparent? Would your literary analysis flow better if you added more transitions between sentences and paragraphs?

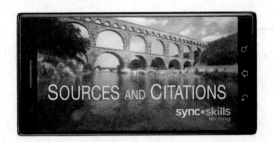

SKILL:
SOURCES AND
CITATIONS

 DEFINE

Sources are the documents and information that an author uses to research his or her writing. Some sources are primary sources, or first-hand accounts of information; others are secondary sources, which are written later and are based on primary sources. Citations give information about the sources an author used to research and write an informative/explanatory text. Citations are required whenever authors quote others' words or refer to others' ideas in their writing. Citations let readers know who originally came up with those words and ideas.

 IDENTIFICATION AND APPLICATION

- Sources can be either primary or secondary. Primary sources are first-hand accounts or original materials, such as the following:

  › Letters or other correspondence
  › Photographs
  › Official documents
  › Diaries or journals
  › Autobiographies or memoirs
  › Eyewitness accounts and interviews
  › Audio recordings and radio broadcasts
  › Literary texts, such as novels, poems, fables, and dramas
  › Works of art
  › Artifacts

- Secondary sources are usually texts. Secondary sources are the written interpretation and analysis of primary source materials. Some examples of secondary sources include:

  › Encyclopedia articles
  › Textbooks
  › Commentary or criticisms

> Histories
> Documentary films
> News analyses
> Biographies, obituaries, eulogies

- Whether sources are primary or secondary, they must be **credible** and **accurate**. This means the information in the sources should be reliable and up-to-date.

- When a writer of a literary analysis quotes directly from a source, he or she must copy the words exactly as they appear in the text, placing them within quotation marks. Here's an example from the student model:

> As Josephson says in paragraph 4, even though it was against the law to hire children younger than 13 to work in factories, "parents often lied about a child's age," and "[m]ill owners "looked the other way, because child labor was cheap."

- Writers of literary analyses must cite, or identify, the sources they're quoting directly. One way to do this is to name the author in the sentence. This is the method shown in the excerpt above. (The writer of the analysis also includes the paragraph number so that readers know exactly where the quoted material can be found in the text.) Another method for citing a source is to put the author's name in parentheses at the end of the sentence in which the quotation appears. Ask your teacher for the method he or she prefers.

- Writers must also provide citations when borrowing ideas from another source, even when writers are just paraphrasing, or putting the ideas into their own words. Citations serve to credit the source and to help readers find out where they can learn more.

 MODEL

In this excerpt from the Student Model, "Mother Jones and Cesar Chavez: Standing Up for Workers' Rights," the writer quotes from the text he or she is analyzing and identifies the sources of each quotation.

> Unlike Josephson, the authors of *About Cesar* are deeply enthusiastic about their subject, Cesar Chavez. In the first paragraph, these authors from the Cesar Chavez Foundation quote Robert F. Kennedy by saying that he called Chavez "**one of the heroic figures of our time.**" They begin their text by introducing Chavez as a "**true American hero,**" a "**farm labor leader . . . a community organizer . . . and a crusader for the environment and consumer**

rights." Later, in paragraph 15, they refer to him as a **"unique and humble leader, as well as a great humanitarian and communicator who influenced and inspired millions of Americans from all walks of life."** Then, in paragraph 19, they call him **"a common man with an uncommon vision."** They support these claims with relevant textual evidence of Chavez's achievements. In paragraph 2, they describe how as a boy, he worked in California's **"fields, orchards, and vineyards, where he was exposed to the hardships and injustices of farm worker life."**

Notice that only the portions of *About Cesar* that are taken directly from the text appear within quotation marks and that the authors of the source text (people from the Cesar Chavez Foundation) are identified in the sentence that contains the quotation. The first quote is particularly tricky because the writer of the model must cite not only the authors of *About Cesar,* but the person whom those authors are quoting—Robert F. Kennedy. Since no embedded citation is included in the remaining quotes, readers can assume that they come directly from the authors of *About Cesar,* and not from an outside source.

 PRACTICE

Write in-text citations for quoted information in your literary analysis essay. When you are finished, trade with a partner and offer each other feedback. How successful was the writer in citing sources for the essay? Offer each other suggestions, and remember that they are most helpful when they are constructive and supportive.

EDIT, PROOFREAD, AND PUBLISH

CA-CCSS: CA.W.7.1a, CA.W.7.1b, CA.W.7.1c, CA.W.7.1d, CA.W.7.1e, CA.W.7.4, CA.W.7.5, CA.W.7.6, CA.W.7.8, CA.W.7.9b, CA.W.7.10, CA.SL.7.1a, CA.SL.7.1c, CA.SL.7.4a, CA.SL.7.6, CA.L.7.1b, CA.L.7.1c, CA.L.7.2a, CA.L.7.2b, CA.L.7.3a, CA.L.7.4b

WRITING PROMPT

Imagine what it would be like to work long hours under dangerous conditions for little pay. Think about how your life would be different if you had to work in a factory or on a farm as a migrant farm worker, instead of going to school. The world is full of injustice, but fortunately, there are people who believe in speaking up for the powerless and defending human rights.

In this unit, you have been reading nonfiction texts about real people who stood up for the rights of others and brought about social change. From Mother Jones, a fierce fighter for child labor laws, to Cesar Chavez, who fought for the rights of ill-treated farm workers, these great people had something in common: They fought for fairness and inspired social change.

Mahatma Gandhi and Nelson Mandela also fought for change. Both Gandhi and Mandela are inspiring, but the texts that you have read about them are very different. Write a literary analysis in which you compare and contrast the text about Gandhi with the text about Mandela to determine which is more convincing in presenting and supporting the claim that this individual was a great defender of justice and human rights. Analyze the reasons and evidence presented in the text as well as the language that is used to describe the individual's words, actions, and accomplishments. Then decide which writer was more persuasive in defending his claim about the impact this person had on human rights.

Your literary analysis should include

- a comparison-contrast of two nonfiction texts you have read in this unit.

WRITING PROMPT *continued*

- an explicitly stated claim about the topic.
- a logically organized presentation of sound reasons and textual evidence.
- a conclusion that sums up your literary analysis of which text was more persuasive and leaves your readers with an original thought about the topic.

Now that you have revised your literary analysis and have received input from your peers, it's time to edit and proofread your writing to produce a final version. Ask yourself these questions: Have I fully supported my claim with strong textual evidence? Is my evidence relevant and sufficient? How well have I cited my sources? Does my literary analysis need more transitions to produce a better connection and flow of ideas? Is my organizational structure clear? How well have I used persuasive language?

Once you are satisfied with your work, proofread it for errors. For example, check that you have used correct punctuation for quotations and citations. Ask yourself if you have capitalized all proper nouns and spelled all words correctly. Have you used commas to set off coordinate adjectives? Have you used precise word choice? Could you have said the same thing using fewer words and less repetitive sentences?

Once you have made all your corrections, you are ready to submit and publish your work. You can give your writing to family and friends, display it in the classroom, or post it online. If you decide to publish it online, include links to your sources and citations. This will enable your readers to learn more from your sources on their own time.

Please note that excerpts and passages in the StudySync® library and this workbook are intended as touchstones to generate interest in an author's work. The excerpts and passages do not substitute for the reading of entire texts, and StudySync® strongly recommends that students seek out and purchase the whole literary or informational work in order to experience it as the author intended. Links to online resellers are available in our digital library. In addition, complete works may be ordered through an authorized reseller by filling out and returning to StudySync® the order form enclosed in this workbook.

Reading & Writing Companion

125

Text Fulfillment
Through StudySync

If you are interested in specific titles, please fill out the form below and we will check availability through our partners.

ORDER DETAILS

Date:

TITLE	AUTHOR	Paperback/ Hardcover	Specific Edition *If Applicable*	Quantity

SHIPPING INFORMATION

Contact:

Title:

School/District:

Address Line 1:

Address Line 2:

Zip or Postal Code:

Phone:

Mobile:

Email:

BILLING INFORMATION ☐ *SAME AS SHIPPING*

Contact:

Title:

School/District:

Address Line 1:

Address Line 2:

Zip or Postal Code:

Phone:

Mobile:

Email:

PAYMENT INFORMATION

☐ CREDIT CARD

Name on Card:

Card Number:

Expiration Date:

Security Code:

☐ PO

Purchase Order Number:

StudySync Text Fulfillment, BookheadEd Learning, LLC
610 Daniel Young Drive | Sonoma, CA 95476